Handbook for
Music
Supervision

Handbook for
Music
Supervision

Dee Hansen

The National Association for Music Education

Published in partnership with
MENC: The National Association for Music Education

Published in the United States of America
By Rowman & Littlefield Education
A Division of Rowman & Littlefield Publishers, Inc.
A wholly owned subsidary of The Rowman & Littlefield Publishing Group, Inc.
4501 Forbes Boulevard, Suite 200, Lanham, Maryland 20706
www.rowmaneducation.com

Estover Road
Plymouth PL6 7PY
United Kingdom

First Rowman & Littlefield Education edition 2007
Copyright © 2002 by MENC: The National Association for Music Education

British Library Cataloguing in Publication Information Available

Library of Congress Control Number: 2002510825

ISBN-13: 978-1-56545-150-6 (pbk. : alk. paper)
ISBN-10: 1-56545-150-3 (pbk. : alk. paper)

♾™ The paper used in this publication meets the minimum requirements of
American National Standard for Information Sciences—Permanence of
Paper for Printed Library Materials, ANSI/NISO Z39.48-1992.
Manufactured in the United States of America

Contents

Introduction

At the 2000 MENC conference in Washington, D.C., the MENC leadership unveiled a long-range plan for the future of music education, Vision 2020.[1] The challenges and future issues discussed by the Vision 2020 authors will directly impact supervisors of music in local and state venues. Supervisors must be able to articulate the need for and purpose of music education; assure quality music programs; successfully communicate with a wide variety of constituents; oversee resources—both financial and instructional; coordinate scheduling, inventory, purchasing, and budgets; direct a vision for the future health of music education; and effectively problem-solve. This breathtaking "spinning of many plates" is indicative of the continual challenges that music supervisors face daily.

Additionally, the ongoing work of aligning local curriculum with the National Standards for Music Education reaches far into the future. Most states have adopted the National Standards, yet implementing their comprehensive scope often requires music teachers to change their philosophies and instruction and succeeds only with the support of parents, administrators, and community. Given the potential shortage of music teachers in the future, supervisors need to guide the delicate balance of recruiting and maintaining teachers while assuring quality programs.

Finally, school reform measures have created an educational environment requiring accountability for student performance in all curriculum areas. Accountability issues on many levels threaten the stability and longevity of music programs. Reports of music programs being shortened or eliminated to make way for longer reading classes are becoming more common. Advocacy efforts have become critical in preserving music offerings. Today's public relations work often finds the music supervisor educating the public about the benefits of music education as it applies to school improvement.

The purpose of this handbook is to provide recommended "best practices" and resources for current and future supervisors of music at the state and K–12 school-district levels. Throughout, the emphasis in each chapter is directed to leadership qualities and successful practices. The intent is not to provide a "how-to" manual, but to give examples of how music supervisors nationwide have effectively dealt with common—and not-so-common—issues and challenges, with special emphasis on leadership, processes and procedures, communication and collaboration, and summary suggestions.

Music supervisors representing each of the six MENC divisions, as well as music supervisors at state departments of education in those divisions, have contributed to this publication. I would like to thank the following district and state supervisors for their time, expertise, and willingness to share specific details of their jobs in the hope of helping others to provide leadership in music education:

Southwestern Division
Marge Banks, district fine arts coordinator, Olathe Public Schools, Olathe, Kansas
Ron Chronister, president, KMEA, Halstead High School, Halstead, KS

North Central Division
Richard Scott, district music coordinator, Lincoln Public Schools, Lincoln, Nebraska
Mel Pontious, supervisor of music, Wisconsin State Department of Education

Eastern Division
Nick Santoro, K–12 supervisor for arts education, East Brunwick Schools, New Jersey
Scott Shuler, arts education consultant, Connecticut State Department of Education

Northwest Division
Gina May, program consultant for visual and performing arts/assessments,
    Washington State Department of Education
Dave Weatherred, district music coordinator, Spokane Public Schools, Washington

Southern Division
Jeannette Crosswhite, director of arts education, Tennessee State Department of
    Education
Carol Crittenden, district music coordinator, Metropolitan Nashville Public Schools

Western Division
Carol Ann Goodson, state fine arts specialist, Utah State Department of Education,
Don Doyle, supervisor of music, Los Angeles County Schools (As of February 2001,
    Don became director of visual and performing arts with the California State
    Department of Education, but was interviewed for his expertise in district
    music supervision.)

I would also like to express my sincere thanks to the following colleagues at the Kansas State Department of Education who provided invaluable advice, expertise, and support: Dale Dennis, deputy commissioner; Ron Nitcher, team leader, finance and budgeting; Kathy Toelkes, public relations; Rod Bieker, legal services; Steve Adams, team leader, school improvement and accreditation team; Jeannette Nobo, team coordinator, school improvement and accreditation team; Kathy Boyer, KSDE staff development specialist; and Jackie Lakin, library media specialist, school improvement and accreditation team.

Additional thanks to Elaine Bernstorf, associate professor of music education and acting associate dean of fine arts at Wichita State University in Kansas, and her graduate students for researching and writing much of the material in Chapter 8; Danny Rocks of Alfred Publishing for providing a comprehensive list of advocacy sources; John Mahlmann, executive director of MENC, for providing current information on strategic planning; Richard Scott, supervisor of music in Lincoln Public Schools, for providing many of the forms found in the appendix; and Eric Hansen (my better half), executive director of the Kansas Library Network Board, for providing current information on Web site development and information about SWOT analysis. Also, I must express my devoted thanks to him for his unflagging support, advice, and patience.

—Dee Hansen

1. Clifford Madsen, ed., *Vision 2020: The Housewright Symposium on the Future of Music Education* (Reston, VA: MENC, 2000).

Chapter 1
Leadership Philosophies

For anyone serving in a supervisory position, exhibiting strong leadership qualities through interaction with other people is critical to success. While some people seem to possess a natural ability to lead, leadership can be learned through pursuing on-the-job education, observing outstanding role models, and listening to one's inner senses when tackling issues. In his book *Managing People Is Like Herding Cats*, Warren Bennis (1997) describes several common traits of good leaders:

1. Leaders must have a strong sense of who they are and what constitutes their own character.
2. Leaders must have a strongly defined sense of purpose—why we do what we do and for whom.
3. Leaders must have the capacity to generate and sustain trust through communication, caring, consistency, and being candid.
4. Leaders must be willing to take action and be willing to learn from their errors. (p. 163)

Qualities of today's strong leaders differ from managerial practices of the past. Increased use of advanced technology to communicate, accelerated workloads and timelines, and the need for buy-in from those who are being led have required that leadership roles change. One example from the field of music supervision is the fact that no longer is it expected that teachers will automatically use a curriculum as "presented" to them. District music supervisors surveyed from around the country indicated that they utilized all teachers in the district to collaborate and write local curricula. State supervisors also utilized teachers as the creators of the state curriculum. See Table 1, Changes in Leadership Practices, for a description of five areas of change from past managerial practices to today's leadership strategies.

In this context of change in leadership behavior, Bennis (1997) also compares managers and leaders:

- The manager administers; the leader innovates.
- The manager is a copy; the leader is an original.
- The manager maintains; the leader develops.
- The manager relies on control; the leader inspires trust.
- The manager has a short-range view; the leader has a long-range perspective.

Table 1. Changes in Leadership Practices		
Leadership Practice	**From the Past**	**To the Future**
Openness to Participation	Our organization values employees listening to the organization's leaders and doing what the leaders tell them to do.	Our organization values employees actively participating in any discussion or decision affecting them.
Openness to Diversity	Our organization values employees falling in line with the overall organizational direction.	Our organization values diversity in perspectives leading to a deeper understanding of organizational reality and an enriched knowledge base for decision making.
Openness to Conflict	Our organization values employees communicating a climate of group harmony and happiness.	Our organization values employees resolving conflict in a healthy way that leads to stronger solutions for complex issues.
Openness to Reflection	Our organization values employees conveying a climate of decisiveness. Firm decisions are made and implemented without looking back.	Our organization values employees reflecting on their own and others' thinking in order to achieve better organizational decisions.
Openness to Mistakes	Our organization values employees concentrating on making no mistakes and working as efficiently as possible.	Our organization values employees acknowledging mistakes and learning from them.

Note. Modified from Jerry Patterson, *Leadership for Tomorrow's Schools* (Alexandria, VA: Association for Supervision and Curriculum Development, 1993), pp. 5–13.

- The manager asks how and when; the leader asks what and why.
- The manager has his or her eye on the bottom line; the leader has his or her eye on the horizon.
- The manager accepts the status quo; the leader challenges it.
- The manager does things right; the leader does the right thing. (p. 63)

When asked what leadership qualities they most admired, the contributing district and state music supervisors around the United States responded with the following list of qualities:

- **Visionary:** While keeping track of many irons in the fire, leaders don't get bogged down with the minutia. They can successfully convey and implement vision.

- **Supportive:** When risks are taken and failure occurs, leaders allow for personal growth of individuals. They can express empathy with those with whom they work.
- **Communicative:** Leaders communicate clearly, promptly, and effectively with others.
- **Joyful:** Leaders show genuine eagerness to work with others and maintain a sense of humor.

Common Responsibilities for Local Supervisors

Local music supervisors share several common tasks including the following:

- leading the development of music curriculum, as well as curriculum development in other fine arts areas
- overseeing the hiring of itinerant staff (teachers who are assigned to more than one building)
- acting as liaison between the music or arts staff and district office leadership.

Some of the other job responsibilities of local music supervisors include hiring and supervising accompanists; budget and planning; equipment repair; arranging transportation for concerts and festivals; city events' management; supervision of conductors, coaches, budgets, and temporary staff for all city events; districtwide visual art and music events oversight; liaison with community arts organizations; community arts events coordination; development of assessment tools; advice on policies and procedures; and possible permanent or substitute teaching responsibilities, as needed. Sample job descriptions for local supervisors are found in Appendix A.

District Policies

Every school district has a written set of policies and procedures, with which district administrators must be familiar. Because of an increasing number of regulations for special education, civil rights, and contractual legalities, many decisions regarding students and teachers depend on the district's policies. These issues will be examined more extensively in Chapter 8.

Communication: Active Listening

All the music supervisors interviewed during the preparation of this handbook emphasized the importance of communication with music teachers, other administrators, and the community. Without strong communication, most efforts fail. In order to collaborate, persons in leadership roles must first effectively communicate. In *The 7 Habits of Highly Effective People*, Stephen Covey (1990) describes the most important component of communication: "Empathic listening gets inside another person's frame of reference. You look out through it, you see the world the way they see the world, you understand their paradigm, you understand how they feel"

Good Communication Skills for Supervisors

- **Communicate regularly** and often with district music (arts) staff. Be visible.
- **Listen with empathy** to others' concerns, issues, and ideas to solve problems and collaborate most effectively.
- **Avoid favoritism**—be fair to all.
- **Avoid overextending** personal resources by trying to do more than is reasonably possible (e.g., trying to attend all music events).
- **Rotate** visits to events according to a system, making sure that staff, parents, and other administrators are informed well in advance.
- **Prioritize** needs and work on "visionary" items at least once a day.
- **Make lists** so as not to forget tasks.
- **Be aware of political issues** and the climate at the district, state, and national levels (e.g., the 2001 energy crisis in California could negatively affect future school program funding). Leadership needs to be proactive in preparation.
- **Delegate**: supervisors are sometimes seen as customer service representatives rather than district administrators. Work regularly on vision rather than focusing exclusively on managing the minutia.
- **Actively educate the community**: sit on committees, initiate contact with decision-makers or program supporters.
- **Think ahead**: be willing to lay the groundwork for future needs.

(p. 240). A good resource for supervisors is Larry Holpp's *The Team Turbo Training Kit: Team Member's Handbooks and Facilitators Guides* (1999), which lists ten elements for effective listening: (1) look for shared interests; (2) base estimations not on presentation, but content; (3) wait until the speaker has finished before responding; (4) listen for ideas as well as facts and allow the speaker to present the ideas in full before questioning them; (5) become proficient in note-taking; keep notes simple and focussed on the ideas; (6) listen physically as well as mentally; (7) get rid of as many distractions as possible; (8) think of listening as a way to learn; (9) remain open to the meanings behind the words; (10) use the time between the speaking and thinking to assess, record thoughts, and formulate questions (sec. 2, p. 22).

The supervisors interviewed had many and varied ways to communicate, but, in most cases, a personal visit was their first choice—either at the school site or in the district office. Face-to-face discussions allow for the most effective empathic listening. The telephone is also a helpful vehicle for one-to-one communication. E-mail works very well for transmitting messages to larger groups of people. Most supervisors were able to e-mail memos to all music staff, eliminating the need for paper communication. However, written communications are still very effective, especially as back-up to e-mail messages. See the Good Communications Skills for Supervisors sidebar for more suggestions.

And finally, keep in mind Peter Senge's definition of "learning organizations," in *The Fifth Discipline: The Art and Practice of the Learning Organization* (1990), as organizations

> where people continually expand their capacity to create the results they truly desire, where new and expansive pattens of thinking are nurtured, where collective aspiration is set free, and where people are continually learning how to learn together. (p. 3)

References

Bennis, W. (1997). *Managing people is like herding cats.* Provo, UT: Executive Excellence Publishing.

Covey, S. R. (1990). *The 7 habits of highly effective people.* New York: Simon and Schuster.

Holpp, L. (1999). *The team turbo training kit: Team member's handbooks and facilitator's guides.* New York: McGraw-Hill.

Senge, Peter M. (1990). *The fifth discipline: The art and practice of the learning organization.* New York: Currency Doubleday.

Chapter 2
Managing People, Paper, and Time

Music supervisors at the district level are challenged by demands that differ from those of their counterparts in other curriculum areas. While most district administrators deal with curriculum and assessment issues, music administrators also take part in the scheduling of concerts and festivals and the rental and repair of musical instruments, among other tasks. In order to assure the smooth management of these responsibilities, music supervisors need to establish a personal system for organizing their work. Stephen Covey's "seven habits to live by" (1990), which foster positive personal and professional behavior, provide sound advice for music supervisors who lead the music teachers in their districts and represent the arts among district leadership. Here is an adaptation of Covey's principles to match music supervision:

- "Be proactive." District and state music supervisors often find themselves putting out fires on a regular basis. Working to solve problems in positive ways, always with an eye to the future, is a critical habit for leaders.
- "Begin with the end in mind." Planning backwards is an excellent exercise that encourages strong goal setting and decisive organizational steps. Whether you are working on a district curriculum or planning concert festivities, it is important to have a vision about what the end product will be.
- "Put first things first." Supervisors must balance important relationships, roles, and activities. Prioritization is a critical attribute of an effective leader. Additionally, delegation of responsibilities empowers others to lead and helps to lighten the burdensome load of supervisory work.
- "Think win/win." Work to find mutually beneficial solutions in a cooperative rather than competitive environment. Creative problem solving often leads to finding solutions that involve new ideas and alternatives.
- "Seek first to understand, then to be understood." As described in Chapter 1, empathetic listening involves listening with understanding first. A good listener is a learner who gathers information and sensitivities before making final decisions.
- "Synergize." Music supervisors often find themselves in the position to value and respect differences, to build on strengths, and to compensate for weaknesses. Arranging for teachers to meet together, exchange ideas, peer tutor, and learn together from others creates an exciting synergy in a school district.

7

- "Sharpen the saw." This habit is best described as taking time to smell the roses. Supervisors must take care of themselves—renew their physical, spiritual, mental and social/emotional parts. Maintaining a balance in life and, specifically, the workplace is critical for personal effectiveness as a leader. (pp. 65–288)

Efficient Time Management

Given the many responsibilities of music supervisors, effective time management is an extremely important tool. Stress is often caused by situations in which too much needs to be done in too little time. Albritton's nine steps (1990) to efficient time management provide a clear list of priorities to follow to avoid losing control:

1. List your goals—both long and short term.
2. Rank your goals as (1) most important; (2) second in importance; and (3) least important. Re-examine the #2 goals and reclassify them as either #1 or #3. Once you have established your #1 goals, discard the others.
3. Set priorities in terms of what you need to do to reach the #1 goals.
4. Make a daily "To Do" list. This can include both work and home.
5. Prioritize your "To Do" list.
6. Continually ask "What is the best use of my time right now?"
7. Handle each piece of paper only once, if possible.
8. Delegate an appropriate amount of the workload.
9. Use the Swiss cheese approach: Take small bites of large projects until they are completed. (p. 123)

District Calendars

Time management and personal and professional habits directly affect the ability to provide leadership. One of the many responsibilities listed by the supervisors interviewed for this book was the development of district calendars. Some music supervisors indicated only advisory responsibilities, while others reported that they are completely responsible for the district music calendars. Depending on the size of the district, the development of an annual calendar ranges from fairly simple to involving a matrix of complexities. Music supervisors must be ready to serve as coordinator and conciliator in this process—they must help problem-solve and find the best solutions for everyone involved. In large districts, it is safe to assume that not everyone will get everything that he or she wants when programs are scheduled. Conflicts between elementary, middle, and high school scheduling are common, especially where families have students in more than one school.

Usually district schedules are set in the spring prior to the targeted school year. Some possible scenarios are as follows:
- Teachers and administrators collaborate on what their scheduling needs are; districtwide events and events associated with district performance venues are entered on a master calendar at the district level. Communication goes out to all

the affected schools via the Internet and superintendent newsletters.

- The district holds a "calendar" day, inviting all those involved in scheduling events that are to be placed on the calendar. A month-by-month discussion occurs, allowing all participants to voice their scheduling needs. Because the calendar day provides an opportunity for everyone's input, few surprises occur during the year in terms of events being scheduled on top of each other. Dates of events are published on the district Web site at the beginning of each school year.

Preparing for Festivals

Most district music supervisors are deeply involved with the planning, organizing, and coordination of music festivals. While any large event may present unforeseen circumstances, careful planning is key to hosting a well-organized festival. Lincoln, Nebraska, music supervisor Richard Scott organizes many of these events each year and has ironed out many bugs in the process (see the checklist in Appendix B). These are some of the processes and procedures that have worked well for him:

- Secure the festival site. Try to secure, if possible, the same dates each year; establish a close working relationship with the athletic or facilities department.
- Gather an accurate, comprehensive mailing list at least six months prior to the event. If the festival is in the fall, have the mailing list ready in early spring of the school year prior to the event.
- In early May, send letters of invitation describing the event, dates and times, entry fees, how the judging system works, and the deadline for entries.
- The entry form attached to the letter should include school name, phone number, e-mail address, classification, number of students in band or choir, whether flags will be judged, and names of teachers and administrators in charge.
- Trophies should be ordered well in advance, and it is better to over-order, just in case more receive a particular rating than expected.
- Hire judges in the spring. Nebraska has changed to a six-judge format for marching bands, making the time needed to secure them all the more critical.
- Make sure all logistics and equipment are provided for well in advance, such as wireless microphones, clipboards, tape recorders, computers with pre-designed spreadsheets for tallying scores, and so on.
- Hire photographers well in advance.
- Hire security personnel to protect gate receipts and concession money.

Block Scheduling

The MENC publication *Scheduling Time for Music* (1995) contains very good resources to assist with block scheduling questions, including an excellent annotated bibliography that points to other books, articles, and studies. One of the publications listed, *High School Restructuring—Block Scheduling: Implications for Music*

Educators, by Larry Blocher and Richard Miles (1996), includes advice on how to become informed and involved and build networks for sharing information. Some of the other publications include examples of various block schedules found around the country.

MENC's Web site (www.menc.org) devotes an entire section to block scheduling and features portions of *Block Scheduling and the Performance-Based Music Program* (Meidl, 1995). This book describes a February–March 1995 comprehensive survey that included music teachers from thirty-two schools in thirteen states. Teachers responded to questions involving the impact of block scheduling on their instruction through a Likert-type survey instrument. The complete results can be found on the Web site, but of greatest interest to supervisors are these responses:

- Sixty-nine percent of music programs surveyed saw a decrease in enrollment in choir, band, or orchestra after moving to block scheduling.
- Sixty-six percent found that the decrease was directly attributed to scheduling conflicts.
- Nineteen percent loved teaching with a block schedule because they had time to get to know students better and accomplish more in rehearsals.
- Sixty-eight percent believed that block scheduling had been detrimental to performance-based music classes (Meidl, 1995).

The study responses concerning block scheduling were mostly unfavorable. Supervisors of districts that are moving to or already implementing block scheduling should monitor the effects carefully and consider offering staff development on effective instructional and management strategies to help prepare teachers effectively. Often districts modify block scheduling if a strong case is made for its alteration. Collecting and reporting quantitative and qualitative data provides the strongest argument for change.

Some current Web sites that address block scheduling include the following: www.collegeboard.com ("Block Schedules and Student Performance on AP Examinations," *The College Board Office of Research and Development Research Notes,* RN-03, May 1998); www.ncpublicschools.org/Accountability/evaluation/block_scheduling/index.html (North Carolina Department of Public Instruction's most recent study on block scheduling); and www.education.umn.edu/carei/blockscheduling ("Block Scheduling," University of Minnesota Center for Applied Research and Educational Improvement).

Working through Conflict

Dealing with situations involving conflict is a normal part of working with people. Conflict can create difficult circumstances that interfere with productivity and program quality. Looking at the four developmental stages of working groups (Holpp, 1999, sec. 4, p. 15) can be of assistance; these stages, which are progressive, may be particularly evident with writing committees (curriculum or assessment) or committess for district scheduling or district festivals:

1. **Forming**—*group comes together:* Committee members are courteous, and differences are underplayed.
2. **Storming**—*group encounters conflict:* Individuals begin to share negative feedback about specifics of workpace, resources, and objectives; conflicts begin to surface.
3. **Norming**—*group familiarized with expectations:* Work proceeds more smoothly; differences usually limited to matters not related to the group's tasks.
4. **Performing**—*group becomes cohesive; produces results without constant supervision:* Conflict comes into play only when members interact with others not belonging to the group.

A few causes of conflict are common. Music supervisors benefit from recognizing these causes and knowing strategies for positive intervention. Each person relates to others differently and approaches tasks in different ways; these differences involve "personal learning styles." Anthony Gregorc (1985) defines "style" as "outer behavior, characteristics, and mannerisms that are symptomatic of the psyche and of particular mental qualities" (p. 7). Bernice McCarthy (1981) describes two steps in the process of learning: (1) how information is taken in, and (2) how information is processed. McCarthy, like many learning-style theorists, has divided learning-style characteristics into four categories:

- Type-one learners "seek personal meaning"; judge things in relation to personal values; function best through social interactions; are cooperative and sociable; and respect authority when it is earned.
- Type-two learners seek "intellectual competence"; judge and verify information through facts; are patient, reflective, and need to be knowledgeable; and follow the lead of the chain of command.
- Type-three learners "seek solutions to problems" primarily through kinesthetic exploration; want to know how things work and need assurance of usefulness and application; are sometimes short on patience and not interested in philosophical issues; and follow authority but work around it if they see a more efficient way.
- Type-four learners "seek hidden possibilities"; function best using instinctual reactions, synthesizing, and exploring; are creative, enthusiastic learners; and tend to do their own thing rather than follow authority. (McCarthy, p. 33)

Individual learning styles emerge when people with diverse learning styles become involved in situations in which they must work together to produce a common product, such as a curriculum or community concert. These differences can cause conflict. Understanding and then respecting each other's differences are enormously useful. Each learning style has its strengths; the group's acknowledgment of these differences and strengths can greatly enhance the quality of the final product.

Work habits involve the pace, orientation to detail, job skills, and flexibility of individuals working in a group. Productivity is affected when these habits are dramatically different among members. The music supervisor must be sensitive to these differences and make adjustments that set minimum requirements for pace and work quality. In some cases, assigning responsibilities in rotation helps to maintain equity among workgroup members.

Teachers work in an environment that is, on one hand, highly regulated and, on the other, very independent. Whether the supervisor works with individual teachers in their buildings or with working groups of teachers, the differences in how individuals cope with challenge become very evident. Many do not wish to make commitments or take risks in the event that the wrong decision might be made; if the decision or direction is wrong, then they seek to place blame on others. Supervisors must help teachers to weigh alternatives and assess consequences. Bringing groups to consensus is important so that everyone stands behind the decision or direction.

Interpersonal Skills

Communication skills involve the ability to listen, provide feedback, give instruction, and convey information. As Holpp explains, the skills that move the group forward and diffuse conflict are fairness, openness, nonjudgmental attitudes, and giving credit where it is due. Conflict, on the other hand, is actively brought on by aggression, personal attacks, suppression of other's opinions, avoidance of cooperative interaction, and dominance (Holpp, 1999, sec. 4, p. 9). By examining the five conflict styles of Robert Garmston and Bruce Wellman (1998), supervisors can identify and assist in directing individuals in conflict into positive and productive action. See the Conflict Styles sidebar for detailed descriptions.

In the early 1990s, when school reform efforts began in earnest, Michael Fullan (1990) described change as consisting of new materials, new behaviors and practices, and new beliefs and understandings. He wrote that change is a complex, ongoing process that

- attempts to help people in a new direction toward a shared vision of improvement
- makes things different, which should be based on carefully established values and managed carefully over an appropriately allocated time
- is inevitable and constant, but should be made to be planned and positive
- moves toward growth and improvement with ownership by the stakeholders
- brings about new ideas, understandings, and practices, leading to meaningful improvements in existing conditions during which people move from one set of beliefs to another
- is developmental, planned, and intensely personal, promoting individual and organizational growth
- is an individual and group process rooted in a vision driven by goals and commitments over time
- is a process in which some factors can be predicted and planned for, while others cannot be, requiring creative response (Fullan, 1990, p. A-16).

Conflict Styles

Integrating: Individuals whose focus is on problem-solving, exchanging information, and reaching solutions acceptable to all parties. People with this style respect divergent points of view and individual differences but may not work well with people who lack commitment to seeking solutions or when deadlines exist.

Obliging: Individuals who place high value on others but not themselves (perhaps a reflection of low self-esteem). This style can be effective when important relationships are at stake but may create further stress for the individual whose self-esteem is at risk.

Dominating: Individuals whose style is the opposite of obliging and whose focus is wholly on self. This person is domineering and often overlooks the needs of others. The dominating style forces others to pay attention to specific issues and is helpful when there is a lack of knowledge or expertise about those issues.

Avoiding: Individuals who place little value on either themselves or others. This style commonly works to avoid issues and withdraw from critical situations, leaving others to struggle with processes and procedures. Avoiding strategies can be useful when time is needed to "cool off" or calm down.

Compromising: Individuals who work to find a middle-of-the-road route to conflict. This style is useful when both sides have merit but can be dangerous when one side is wrong. Compromise works when all parties agree to give up something in order to gain a viable solution.

Note. Summarized from Robert Garmston and Bruce Wellman, *The Adaptive School: Developing and Facilitating Collaborative Groups* (El Dorado Hills, CA: Four Hats Press, 1998), p. 112.

A music supervisor may encounter situations in which the music teachers in his or her district resist change. District administration changes can lead to policy changes that can affect music programs, such as moving from seven- or eight-period days to block scheduling or taking a different direction in curricula and assessments. Building principals may institute policies that alter the way a music teacher would normally interact with other teachers, parents, or students. The supervisor may be involved in helping such teachers to meet conflict in the least resistant and most positive way. Fullan (1990, p. A-22) and Fullan and Hargreaves (1991, p. B-29) suggest strategies for facilitating change in order to diminish conflict:

- Develop a documented change strategy including timeline, resources, and staff development needed. Note gaps between where you are now and where you want to be.
- Decide what steps are needed to move the district or teachers to your vision. Examine those issues or situations that could help or hinder.

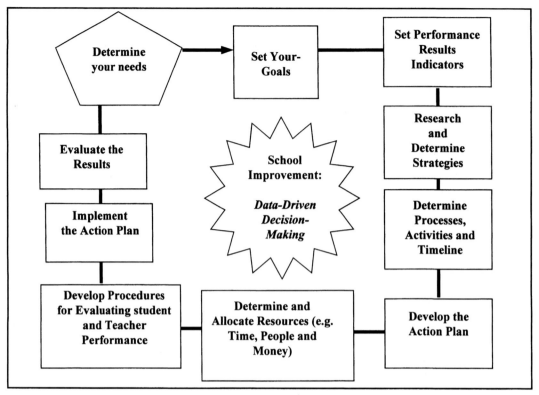

Figure 1. School Improvement

- Engage in consensus building at the district and building levels.
- Assure all teachers that they will receive adequate technical assistance and professional development.
- Focus on building collaborative work cultures in the school and community.

Dealing with School Improvement

Most states, in order to receive federal funds, have developed a comprehensive school improvement system of accountability. At the heart of school improvement are several "non-negotiables," including assessment of student progress, data analysis, long- and short-term planning, and action plans. Accountability systems rely on student data to drive the process. Testing, whether it is through state, local, or national norm-reference assessments, has become the major provider of data. Some states, such as Kansas, also require schools to track such information as student attendance, violent acts, and the percentage of graduating students. Data on students at the district or building level is then analyzed. This information provides a roadmap that helps schools design school improvement plans and policy decisions for the future. See Figure 1, The School Improvement Process, for a schematic that summarizes these points.

Lezotte and Jacoby (1992) describe seven operational characteristics that seem to be present in schools that could be called "effective":

1. strong instructional leadership
2. a clear and focused mission
3. a climate of high expectations for success for all students
4. a safe, orderly environment
5. the opportunity to learn and adequate time spent on academic tasks
6. frequent monitoring of student progress
7. positive home-school relations. (p. 10)

Because most of the data gathered on students for the purposes of school improvement is based on reading, writing, and mathematics testing, specialist teachers (such as those in music, art, and physical education) doubt their involvement in the process. Specialist teachers are often not regarded by administrators or other teachers as a significant factor in improving scores. In truth, the contributions of every teacher are necessary in order to reach the learning needs of every student. In light of this situation, music supervisors need to help teachers understand the importance of their contributions to student learning. The publication *tARgeTS* for Kansas arts educators, updated annually by Hansen (2001), includes instructional strategies and explanations of how to support the school improvement process without sacrificing the teaching of arts content.

Suggestions for Specific Management Tasks

Here are some tips for developing district calendars:

- Schedule calendars as early as possible.
- Consider the needs of teachers and students above all else.
- Utilize capable clerical help and collaborate with district facilitating teachers, if available.
- Whenever possible, duplicate programs (offer the same programs more than once for very large districts).
- Work with district officials to coordinate scheduling issues, conflicts, and needs.
- Include a monthly "newsletter" to music teachers and principals that lists all programs for the next month. This can be both hard copy and electronic.
- Use Web sites, newsletters, e-mail, and local newspapers to publicize calendar events.
- Verify the accuracy of information presented to the public before it leaves the office. If the information is reported incorrectly, have changes made public immediately.

These itemized suggestions are designed to facilitate more efficient time management:

- Look for the most positive ways to view difficult situations.
- Don't procrastinate—prioritize lists of tasks and work to give them closure.
- Delegate responsibilities to others. Some districts have teachers who receive

stipends for assisting with administrative work. Use them if you have them.
- Carry and use a planner or a palm organizer.
- Have communications proofread—be accurate with information shared with others.
- Make sure that the information others report is also accurate—report corrections immediately.

Block scheduling issues can benefit from the pointers listed here:
- Be very involved in scheduling changes at the district level.
- Listen to teachers' concerns; communicate them to the decision-makers.
- Be proactive: educate yourself and your teachers about different block scheduling alternatives.
- Be positive: while scheduling changes can be difficult, some block scheduling formulas have improved and advanced music programs.
- If modifications are needed for scheduling, collect data that demonstrate why change is needed.

Finally, school improvement programs can be approached with these ideas in mind:
- Understand district expectations regarding arts teachers' involvement in the school improvement process.
- Encourage teachers to become aware of and practice the instructional strategies in general education used to improve students' reading, mathematics, and writing abilities. These strategies are highly transferable to the arts and often make excellent teaching strategies.
- Work to advocate for the arts as integral to student learning—music and art used as tools for teaching, as well as content-specific art and music, are critical to the improvement of student academic achievement.
- Encourage teachers to participate in, support, and lead school improvement efforts.

References

Albritton, Rosie L., & Shaughnessy, Thomas W. (1990). *Developing leadership skills: A source book for librarians.* Englewood, CO: Libraries Unlimited.

Blocher, L., & Miles, R. (1996). *High school restructuring—Block scheduling: Implications for music educators.* Springfield, IL: Focus on Excellence.

Covey, S. R. (1990). *The 7 habits of highly effective people.* New York: Simon & Schuster.

Fullan, M. (1990). *Managing change.* Toronto, Canada: University of Toronto Press.

Fullan, M., & Hargreaves, M. (1991). *Guidelines for action: What's worth fighting for in your school.* Canada: Ontario Public School Teacher's Federation.

Garmston, R., & Wellman, B. (1998). *The adaptive school: Developing and facilitating collaborative groups.* El Dorado Hills, CA: Four Hats Press.

Gregorc, A. F. (1985). *Inside styles: Beyond the basics.* Columbia, CT: Gregorc Associates.

Hansen, D., ed. (2001). *tARgeTS.* (For further information, contact Kansas Department of Education, 120 S.E. 10th St., Topeka, KS 66601)

Holpp, L. (1999). *The team turbo training kit.* New York: McGraw-Hill.

Lezotte, L., & Jacoby, B. (1992). *Sustainable school reform: The district context for school improvement.* Okemos, MI: Effective School Products.

McCarthy, B. (1987). *The 4MAT system: Teaching to learning styles with right/left mode techniques* Barrington, IL: Excel.

Meidl, K. (1995). *Block scheduling and the performance-based music program.* (For further information, fax 414-832-6239 or e-mail kmeidl@aol.com)

MENC. (1995). *Scheduling time for music.* Reston, VA: Author.

Chapter 3
Curriculum and Assessment

Leadership in curriculum development involves actively moving schools forward to develop a "learning program that is vigorous and relevant in preparing students for a successful future and that demonstrates results over time" (Gross, 1998, p. xii). The music supervisor's single most important responsibility is facilitating the writing of district curriculum. Teaching in a district without curriculum is like traveling cross-country without a map. Sound curricula that focus and guide the district assure that every student will know and do the agreed-upon essential skills without overlaps or gaps in year-to-year instruction. Implementation of a good curriculum is the basis for successful school reform measures—the catalyst for what should be taught, when it should be taught, what should be assessed, and what professional development ensures effective teaching.

Music educators are fortunate that the National Standards for Music Education (Consortium of National Arts Education Associations, 1994) have been so widely accepted and adopted throughout the country, providing a critical framework for developing student skills and knowledge. In many states, the National Standards have galvanized curriculum development efforts at the local level, as well as state standards and framework development at the state level. The chart in Figure 1 (Systemic Alignment Chart) demonstrates the systemic links between the National Standards, district goals and exit outcomes, development of local curriculum (including benchmarks, objectives and/or indicators), scope-and-sequence, consideration of resources, instructional strategies, professional development, and the teacher/program evaluation process. When a school district plans its curriculum, the interaction of all elements in the process must be considered—from the overall content structure provided by the Standards to the realities of what students and teachers do in the classroom and the methodologies for assessing their work.

It is incumbent upon music supervisors to understand and to help their teachers understand the systems process. Each component of the process affects the others. The curriculum itself will not be a useful tool unless resources, such as money, time, and training, are provided to help teachers acquire the pedagogical and knowledge-based skills needed to effectively implement the curriculum. Evaluation of teachers and programs, coupled with an analysis of student assessment (including performances, self-reflections in journals, traditional pencil-and-paper tests, etc.), inform the curriculum and, in turn, affect future teacher preparation and sub-

19

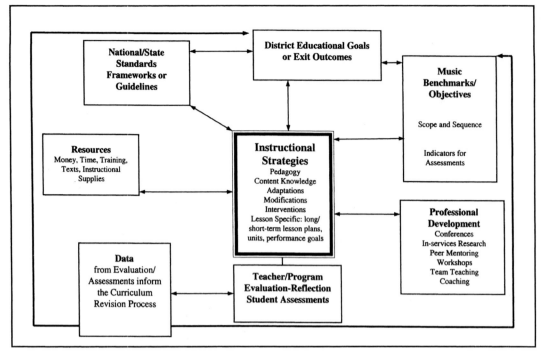

Figure 1. Systemic Alignment Chart

sequent classroom instructional strategies for all students (including special needs, at-risk, and limited English speakers). Be sure to consult the Assessment Terms Glossary sidebar for assistance with terminology.

Describing the Curriculum

School districts generally find their curriculum somewhere along a continuum of four categories:

Not in Place—Beginning to Develop—Completing Development—Implementing

The Curriculum Checklist (see Table 1) can be used as a self-assessment in determining where a district falls in terms of curriculum. All of the self-assessment questions are found as components in the Systemic Alignment Chart (see Figure 1).

The Standards Movement

Since the mid-1990s, our school systems have been adopting a standards-based approach to curriculum development. Educators have questioned the effectiveness of past curricula in meeting the needs of all learners. Information technology, increases in the complexity and interdependence of the today's workplace, and the need for workers to be able to think creatively and problem-solve have led to more specificity in curriculum development, alignment, and assessment. Spencer Kagan (2000) describes eight common themes of the standards movement, with added annotations that outline ways in which those themes are connected to music instruction:

1. *Teach for understanding: thinking, not rote memorization.* While memorization of music for performance is often expected, the cognitive growth in this theme relates to the student's comprehension of the elements in the musical literature itself: cultural and historical background, connections to other curriculum areas, and the implications of how this knowledge affects performance practices. Successful performance not only relies on accurate musical representation of the score, but a deep, well-rehearsed understanding of the intricate musical tapestry.

2. *Cultivate positive attitudes, engagement, and joy with the curriculum.* Music learning prepares students to become lifelong, joyful learners in many walks of life. Students learn to work together with others toward a common goal, to listen and respect their own and others' contributions to the success of a performance or learning experience, and to think independently and interdependently.

3. *Foster a process orientation through ongoing learning cycles.* Music learning often involves sequential patterns of skill and knowledge development. While no prescribed order can be set for developing music skills, most curricula define benchmark levels for attaining these skills, given appropriate instruction time. Music learning is a long, involved, and intensely personal process.

4. *Develop communication skills.* These skills are thought to be primary to workplace success. Music learning provides students with a training ground for articulating clearly and expressively. As an aural art, the function of music performance is to communicate the composer's intent and/or the performer's interpretation. Communication is at the heart of every music experience.

5. *Broaden the curriculum through multiple sources and multiple approaches.* Music learning comes in many shapes and forms. Students can sing or play many different types of instruments and learn about musical literature, musical styles, and genres. Multiple sources and approaches are inherent in music learning.

6. *Integrate instruction though interdisciplinary connections.* National Standards 7, 8, and 9 refer to analyzing and learning about cross-disciplinary connections. Comprehensive music instruction naturally includes these Standards.

7. *Emphasize environmental/social/civic issues and responsibilities.* While environmental responsibilities may not be at issue in a music class, certainly social and civic responsibilities are undertaken in authentic ways every day in class and in performances. One of the many lessons of music education is to accept responsibility for the individual's contribution to the whole, including the student's responsibility to perform a part correctly, work together to create a quality performance, and behave with dignity in and out of the school building for programs and performances.

8. *Emphasize technological literacy.* Technological advances have opened doors to new and exciting opportunities for students to compose, arrange, and perform music. Learning to utilize music software is not only engaging for students, but also provides practice that hones computer skills.

Table 1. Curriculum Checklist

Category *District/Building Systemic Considerations*	Not in Place	Beginning to Develop/ Revise	Completing Development/ Revision	Imple- menting
1. Do we have a districtwide curricula adopted by the local board of education?				
2. Does our curriculum have district learner exit outcomes, goals, or objectives?				
3. Does our curriculum have clearly established local standards, benchmarks, and indicators that align to state or National Standards?				
4. Have we written a comprehensive scope-and-sequence that addresses the knowledge, skills, and applications to be mastered at specified grade levels or courses?				
5. Do all of our K–12 teaching staff for each curriculum area collaborate and agree on the development and implementation of our curriculum?				
6. Do we assure that our curriculum is vertically and horizontally aligned K–12?				
7. Do our district and building leaders support the curriculum?				
Resources				
1. Does our district act on teacher requests for resources (money, time, texts, etc.) that support the curriculum?				
2. Do we have a professional resource center in place that supports instruction across the curriculum?				
3. Do we have a process in place for evaluating, acquiring, and promoting necessary resources in order to meet the learning needs of all students?				
4. Do we have access to electronic networks and resource-sharing systems that expand our access to worldwide information?				
Learning Needs				
1. Does the instruction of our curriculum address the learning needs of all students, including ESL, at-risk, and students with disabilities?				

Category *Learning Needs*	Not in Place	Beginning to Develop/ Revise	Completing Development/ Revision	Imple-menting
2. Do we work to address the learning needs of students with diverse learning styles, multiple intelligences, modifications, adaptations, etc.?				
3. Is the cultural content of our curriculum relevant to our community and students?				
4. Does our curriculum integrate appropriate social and cultural aspects that are different from ours?				
5. Have our instructional materials and curriculum been reviewed for bias or historical inaccuracy?				
Student Assessment				
1. Do we have multiple assessments in place to evaluate the progress of students and identify students not meeting the standards defined in the curriculum?				
2. Have we designed formative and summative assessments linked to curriculum and instruction?				
3. Do we use diverse assessment strategies that best evaluate the progress of our learners?				
4. Are our assessments aligned with our curriculum?				
5. Are our assessments used to improve instruction, assess progress of students, and determine the effectiveness of our curriculum?				
Professional Development				
1. Are our teachers adequately trained to implement our curriculum?				
2. Are we trained to implement accommodations, modifications, and teaching strategies for ESL, special needs, and at-risk students?				
3. Do our professional development opportunities meet our personal teaching needs, as well as our district school reform goals?				
4. Is there alignment between our district goals, curriculum, assessments, and professional development?				

Assessment Terms Glossary

Assessment: A variety of methods and techniques used by educators to measure student knowledge, skills, and other traits in a specific area; a process of gathering data and putting it into an interpretable form for making an evaluative judgment or decision about a student, program, or school. This term also applies generally to tests which measure student learning.

Benchmark: A specific statement of what a student should know and be able to do at a specified time in his or her schooling. Benchmarks are used to measure a student's progress toward meeting a standard.

Criterion-Referenced Assessment: A test or other assessment method designed to measure how well each student attains the specified knowledge/skills within the district/school curriculum; test items are linked to specific objectives, and scores are interpreted in terms of those objectives. The results have meaning in relation to what the student knows or is able to do (rather than on the student in relation to a reference group, as in a norm-referenced test).

Curriculum Standards: Descriptions of what students should know and be able to do in specific content areas.

Evaluation: The careful examination and judging of persons, organizations, or things in relation to stated objectives, standards, or criteria. Within a school improvement process, the school evaluates its progress toward achieving the targeted improvement plan outcomes. Formative evaluation occurs during a process; summative evaluation occurs upon completion of a process.

Indicator: A statement of knowledge or skills that a student demonstrates in order to meet the benchmark; critical to understanding the standards and benchmarks and intended to be met by all students.

Instructional Strategies: Plans of action designed and used by educators to maximize student learning and achievement of desired outcomes. The selection of strategies is based upon the nature of the outcomes and students' learning styles and needs. Research needs to be reviewed to determine the best strategies for improving student learning and performance.

Local Indicators: Measures that give information on the status of the school in achieving improvement goals/targets. Local indicators are measures the school and/or district have selected to demonstrate progress toward improvement goals/targets and should be aligned to the curriculum being implemented. While it may be possible for schools to discover published tests that are aligned with local curricula, indicators developed locally to specifically reflect the local curriculum can have significantly more power in effectively measuring improvement.

Needs Assessment: Self evaluation in the school improvement process conducted by each school and/or district for the purposes of identifying needs and deciding on priorities.

Performance Assessment: An assessment form based on observation and professional judgment requiring students to produce work or engage in direct demonstrations of their skills, understanding, or knowledge using clearly defined criteria; as such, they are a direct measure of what students know and can do. Examples include, but are not limited to, portfolios, direct writing assessments, projects, exhibitions, demonstrations, and simulations.

Portfolio (Assessment): A systematic, organized, and interrelated collection of a student's work that exhibits to the student, parent, teacher, and others the student's efforts, progress, and achievement over time. The student participates in the selection of portfolio contents, selection criteria, judgment for merit criteria, and evidence of self-reflection.

continued on next page

Leadership Roles in Curriculum Development

A music supervisor's responsibilities in overseeing curriculum development are many; nearly all the supervisors interviewed listed these functions:

- Advise the school board about the content, progress, and completion of the district curriculum.
- Participate in long-range planning procedures for music offerings and curriculum writing, including budget issues and timelines.
- Select writers or teachers to facilitate writing committees.
- Oversee the logistics of meetings.
- Submit proposals, make reports, secure resources, and schedule and facilitate meetings.
- Review, synthesize, and share with teaching staff current research and national trends.
- Assist teachers with understanding systemic connections between National Standards, district curriculum, professional development, and assessment and evaluations.
- Develop and analyze data collection forms (input from teachers, e.g., what is being taught by grade, the overlaps, and gaps).
- Guide teachers to agree on both vertical and horizontal alignment of the curriculum.
- Develop materials as a result of teacher curriculum work: scope-and-sequence charts, grade-level objectives, assessment, resources recommendations, and so forth.
- Oversee the selection of new texts, software, music literature, and so forth.
- Evaluate curriculum processes, procedures, and products.

Curriculum Alignment

Many processes must occur in order to develop and implement a quality curriculum. Most importantly, curriculum development should always be organized in a K–12 progression. Alignment problems abound when elementary teachers develop their curriculum separately from the high school staff. Planning and organizing the work of curriculum development may include many of the following tasks:

1. Organizing writing committees and task forces. Large school districts, such as in Olathe, Kansas, have found that teacher facilitators are extremely beneficial to the curriculum development and implementation process. In Olathe, teachers apply to be facilitators for a two- to three-year rotation. The applicants are screened and selected by district personnel. The teacher/facilitator has normal teaching responsibilities but is paid a stipend for organizing his or her peers in curriculum-writing sessions, leading sessions, preparing drafts, and reporting back to the district music supervisor. The facilitators work closely with the district to assure that the groups for whom they are responsible are aligning their work with the district mission, vision, exit outcomes, and objectives.

In order for district music curriculum to be most beneficial, all district staff must participate in the curriculum-writing process. Jacobs (1997) promotes a process called "Curriculum Mapping" that has proven successful in acquiring the participation of all teachers in a district. Steps in his mapping process are as follows:

- Data is collected: At a "macro" level, determine and document essential concepts and topics, processes, skills, products, and performances for every teacher. These are referred to as "maps."
- Maps are shared across content areas in every building: teachers look for repetitions, gaps, meaningful assessments, alignment with standards, potential areas for integration, and timeliness.
- In a small group (six to eight), teachers who do not normally work together review the maps individually; a reporting follows. This group identifies "red-flag" areas that need further attention.
- General and specific comments are reviewed by all members of the building faculty: The optimum size for future working groups is identified. Specialist teachers, in areas such as fine arts, physical education, library, and media, work with other district schools that feed into the same middle school and high school. At these meetings, the same procedures are followed as in the building meetings. Gaps, repetitions, potential assessments, and alignment to standards are checked.
- The entire faculty in a building (for specialists, smaller groups of teachers from the feeder schools) work to edit, revise, and negotiate the scope-and-sequence of the curriculum. Care is taken to describe skills and processes in developmentally appropriate levels. Teachers for each curriculum area create essential questions that help to clarify, organize, and focus the curriculum. Students participate in developing essential questions as well.
- Discussion moves to the district level, K–12, in all curriculum areas; significant time for research is needed to draw together and analyze the maps of all buildings (or of the feeder school specialists). Completion of the curriculum is often done in summer workshops and faculty meetings led by a task force or curriculum cabinet. (pp. 17–23)

2. Sample resource materials needed for a curriculum-writing committee. Teachers need these to develop a knowledge base for their writing. The music supervisor gathers research and documents to guide the teachers' work. The following materials should be dealt with prior to any writing: National Standards for Music Education; existing state frameworks or guidelines; district educational goals, exit outcomes, mission statement, and vision for the curriculum; exemplary curricula from other states or school districts; research on teaching and learning in music; research on child and adolescent development, including special needs students (such as children who are limited in their English proficiency); high-quality commercially produced learning materials; a district template for the curriculum (if available); state reform goals; and supervisor and teacher recommendations.

3. *Potential components of a curriculum.* The following list provides an example of appropriate components of a district curriculum, although other items may be included that address individual community needs: district mission and goals; district goals, objectives, or outcomes of the music department; curriculum benchmarks and/or objectives; a summary of the document's structure, use, and research/philosophical basis; links to National and state standards; links to state school reform components; indicators for evaluation/assessment; teaching strategies or suggestions for instruction; assessments; scope-and-sequence (recurring components that become strands throughout grade levels and courses); list of materials (both professional and commercial) that can be incorporated into the instruction; glossary; and an acknowledgment section. (See Appendix D for an example of the format for a Standards-based curriculum.)

4. *Public disclosure.* Most school districts require that the board of education approve any newly developed curriculum. The presentation to the board is an excellent opportunity to advocate for music education, as well as inform the general public about the strength and comprehensive nature of the district's music programs.

5. *Rotation of curriculum development.* Many states and districts require a mandatory rotation of curriculum development. Generally, the revision process takes place every five to seven years. "It's never done!" seems to be a common theme of experienced staff who have experienced the process several times. Though intense and time-consuming, the curriculum-writing process is one of the most powerful staff development opportunities available. The conversations, idea-sharing, revisiting what should be emphasized, and individual talents and strengths of teachers as potential mentors for others are irreplaceable.

6. *Development of sample assessments.* Assessments in music are often described as "performance-based." Music educators are most concerned that their students be able to perform, create, analyze, or describe music, not simply restate facts. Performance assessments are also called "constructed-responses" because students are not provided with specific choices for answers. At the other end of the continuum are "selected-responses," because students must choose the appropriate response from the answers provided. Figure 2, Assessment Tools Continuum, presents a schematic for the continuum of assessment tools commonly used in the music classroom.

Student self-reflection—the verbal or written expression of an informed opinion—is becoming very common. Howard Gardner's Arts PROPEL model for music

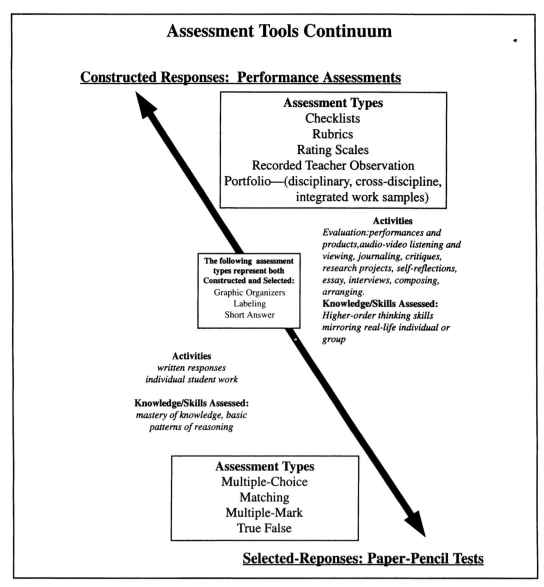

Assessment Tools Continuum

Constructed Responses: Performance Assessments

Assessment Types
Checklists
Rubrics
Rating Scales
Recorded Teacher Observation
Portfolio—(disciplinary, cross-discipline,
integrated work samples)

Activities
*Evaluation:performances and
products,audio-video listening and
viewing, journaling, critiques,
research projects, self-reflections,
essay, interviews, composing,
arranging.*
Knowledge/Skills Assessed:
*Higher-order thinking skills
mirroring real-life individual or
group*

The following assessment
types represent both
Constructed and Selected:
Graphic Organizers
Labeling
Short Answer

Activities
*written responses
individual student work*

Knowledge/Skills Assessed:
*mastery of knowledge, basic
patterns of reasoning*

Assessment Types
Multiple-Choice
Matching
Multiple-Mark
True False

Selected-Reponses: Paper-Pencil Tests

Figure 2. Assessment Tools Continuum

(1992) provides a wealth of examples for self-reflection. PROPEL is an acronym for Production, Performance, and Reflection.

7. *Modifications and adaptations for special needs students.* The Individuals with Disabilities Education Act (IDEA) of 1997, which strengthened and clarified for educational needs the foundation laid by the Americans with Disabilities Act (ADA) of 1990, has created new educational challenges for local school districts. For example, IDEA urges local educators to improve academic progress for students with disabilities by requiring schools to provide access to the general curriculum. IDEA requires, as ADA did, that states ensure that schools are appropriately implementing federal and

state laws and regulations so that students with disabilities are provided a free, appropriate public education in the least restrictive environment. However, IDEA shifted the focus to determining the effectiveness of educational supports and services in meeting the needs of students with disabilities (and, in some states, this includes giftedness). The effectiveness of special education services is measured by the ongoing process of identifying gaps between the current results achieved by schools and the desired outcomes. Identifying these gaps facilitates the development of strategies to address them and move schools closer to the effective implementation of IDEA.

As a result of these requirements, the likelihood has increased that students with special needs will be included in a general music classroom. The January 2001 *Music Educators Journal*, a special focus issue on inclusion, includes extremely helpful articles that should be read and discussed by district music personnel. In addition, Judith Jellison (1979, 1983, 1999, 2000) has written extensively concerning guidelines that assist music teachers with special needs students. For a summary of her presentation to the twelfth National Symposium on Research in Music Behavior, see the Principles for the Inclusive Music Classroom sidebar. Linda Damer (2001) states that "music educators who teach in inclusive schools must become part of the collaborative process and not allow themselves to be left out of the team" (p. 22). The music supervisor can provide the encouragement and technical information needed so that teachers can fully participate in the education of all students.

Professional Development

A district budget for professional development hinges on the effectiveness of past efforts. If teachers have been told to attend a district staff development session that did not closely meet their personal needs, the time spent could be considered merely seat time. Convincing a school board and district financial staff that those practices should continue may be difficult, given constant budget constraints. The effectiveness of staff development efforts should be considered throughout the process of curriculum development—from the earliest organizational meetings. Questions to be considered include: "Based on our curriculum, what improvements in student learning and performance are needed?" "What types of professional development are required to make those improvements?" and "How do we know if professional development led to those improvements?" Guskey (1997) describes three principles common to effective staff development efforts:

1. A clear focus on learning and learners. Resources spent on professional development should relate to the school or district mission that emphasizes worthwhile student learning as the principal goal. Teachers should report that staff development activities are well-designed, provide ways to improve their pedagogical skills, and offer multiple approaches for reaching the needs of all students.

2. Focus on both individual and organizational change. The music supervisor can help create change in schools by guiding administrators and teachers in understanding the process of change. Ideally, administrators should initiate discussions about

Principles for the Inclusive Music Classroom

Normalization: Daily life experiences and activities should be as close to cultural norms as possible. If adaptations are needed, they should be minimal.

Social image: Students with disabilities should be helped to shine in their classrooms.

Chronological age appropriateness: Tasks and instruction should be structured so that skills learned are based on chronological age, not mental or emotional age.

Transition: Students should learn skills that can be transferred to other life experiences.

Functional value: Students should learn skills that help them make the transition into adulthood or parallel situations in real life.

Participation and partial participation: Students should have opportunities to participate as much as possible in classroom activities.

Individual achievement and choice: As an important component of the IDEA legislation, students should have opportunities to achieve functional academic and social objectives, to reach personal goals, and to express individual choices.

Collaboration and support system: Because a basic assumption of the law is that no individual teacher has the expertise to meet all of the educational needs of all students, music teachers should collaborate and communicate with building and district support teams to get assistance in providing the maximum music experience for all students.

Note. Summarized from J. A. Jellison, (2001, February), *Inclusive Strategies for All Learners,* Paper presented at the Kansas Music Educators Conference, Wichita, KS.

curriculum and instructional matters on a regular basis. They should encourage "participation and nurture a school environment that fosters learning, experimentation, cooperation, and professional respect" (Fullan, Bennett, & Rolheiser-Bennett, 1989; Little, 1982). Teachers need time to observe each other as professionals and for self-reflection and preparation. The success of a curriculum relies heavily on how well it is implemented in the classroom and across the district. Without adequate teacher training, systemic alignment will not occur.

3. *Make small changes guided by a grand vision.* "Think big, but start small" (Guskey, 1995, p. 7). Incremental changes must be guided by a larger vision that focuses on the learners—both students and teachers. Change and improvement require a sustained, goal-driven process that focuses on best practices.

Results-Based Staff Development

In Kansas, the statewide model, *Results-Based Staff Development* (Kansas State Department of Education, 1998), is conceived on a five-point continuum both at the district- and the building-level. Staff development must relate to building and district academic goals. Teachers are given professional development points and, ultimately, salary-scale advancements based on the level of implementation they have achieved at the in-services or workshops they have attended. The entire process is inextricably linked to the accreditation of individual buildings within a district. Principals must report each year how their teachers are placed on a five-level continuum as follows:

Level 1/Non-Use: personnel who have not yet learned about the staff development priority.

Level 2/Awareness: personnel with enough knowledge of the staff development priority to describe, discuss, or explain what it is.

Level 3/Demonstration: personnel with experience using strategies for student learning and school improvement.

Level 4/Integration: personnel who can correlate strategies to student learning and school improvement. Schools at this level have a learning community in which all members understand the staff development priority and practice the strategies.

Level 5/Transfer: personnel who have developed a sense of expertise and confidence and can anticipate needs for school improvement, identify staff development priorities, and apply appropriate strategies. Staff at this level are able to train and mentor others.

Collaboration and Communication

In most instances, music supervisors are responsible for assisting with the organization and planning of the curriculum-writing process. Glatthorn (1994) has condensed the list above of curriculum development components into four stages of curriculum development: (1) planning: appointing task forces, developing the knowledge base, orienting teachers, developing benchmarks and indicators, and collecting data and input from teachers; (2) production: the actual manufacture of materials, making scope-and-sequence charts, developing curriculum guides, and creating other materials required to support the curriculum; (3) piloting: all activities necessary to use the new materials on a test basis; and (4) implementation: curriculum is in place and being used (pp. 13–15). In each of these phases of curriculum development, the music supervisor is continually communicating and collaborating with teaching staff, district administration, and the community.

One important aspect of collaboration is working with professional artists and arts organizations. Many communities have local arts agencies that engage local or out-of-town visual and performing artists for cultural enrichment. Organizations such as Young Audiences, Inc., encourage professional artists to work with teachers and students in local schools—not to replace the sequential instruction provided by certified arts educators but to provide in-depth experiences in a particular genre, concept, or skill development in the arts. Professional artists work with teachers to match their particular expertise with curricular needs. For instance, if an American history unit on the Civil War is planned for fifth-grade students, the school may decide to employ an artist who specializes in tapestries or songs of that era. Or a jazz musician or professional jazz ensemble may be asked to work with the jazz band or perform for students studying American jazz.

Professional artists, who have honed their skills, are a model and inspiration to students and can engage students in ways that recordings or videotapes cannot match. To connect with sources for finding artists, check with state art agencies or these national arts agencies: National Endowment for the Arts (//arts.endow.gov); National Assembly of State Arts Agencies (www.nassa-arts.org); Arts Education Partnership (//aep-arts.org); ArtsEdge curriculum plans (//artsedge.kennedy-center.org); and Young Audiences, Inc. (www.youngaudiences.org).

Suggestions for Supervising Curriculum Development

In dealing with the nuts and bolts, these tips may provide some avenues for better planning and for enjoying the process more:
- Create curriculum with **all** district staff (not just a committee).
- Identify gaps and repetitions in existing local curriculum (i.e., what is missing according to the National Standards, what is being repeated unnecessarily).
- Align with state and National Standards and state frameworks or guidelines.
- Include links to state reform goals.
- Include suggestions for Special Education/English as a Second Language.
- Look for potential places to integrate with other curriculum areas.
- Create meaningful statements about what you think your students should know and be able to do—the essentials.
- Create a focused scope-and-sequence based on the essentials.
- Suggest places for assessment and evaluation and provide some examples.
- Consider a curriculum as a dynamic, never static, document. Once done, continue to work on how to teach it and to evaluate its effectiveness.
- Enjoy the discussions—talking to each other is the best part!
- Consider including the services of professional artists and performing organizations as part of the implementation of the curriculum.

References

Americans with Disabilities Act of 1990, Pub. L. No. 101-336, 42 U.S.C. § 12101 *et seq.*

Consortium of National Arts Education Associations. (1994). *National standards for arts education.* Reston, VA: MENC.

Damer, Linda K. (Special guest ed.). (2001, January). Inclusion [Special issue]. *Music Educators Journal, 87* (4).

Damer, Linda K. (2001). Inclusion and the law. *Music Educators Journal, 87* (4), 19–22.

Fullan, M. G., Bennett, B., & Rolheiser-Bennett, C. (1989). Linking classroom and school improvement. Paper presented at the meeting of the American Educational Research Association, San Francisco, CA.

Gardner, Howard. (1992). *Arts PROPEL: A handbook for music.* Boston, MA: Educational Testing Service and the President and Fellows of Harvard College.

Glatthorn, A. A. (1994). *Developing a quality curriculum.* Alexandria, VA: National Association for Supervision and Curriculum Development.

Gross, Steven J. (1998). *Staying centered: Curriculum leadership in a turbulent era.* Alexandria, VA: Association for Supervision and Curriculum Development.

Guskey, T. R. (1995). Results-oriented professional development: In search of an optimal mix of effective practices. *Journal of Staff Development, 15* (4), 42–50.

Guskey, T. R. (1997). Research needs to link professionl development and student learning. *Journal of Staff Development, 18* (2), 36–40.

Individuals with Disabilities Education Act (IDEA) of 1997, Pub. L. No. 105-17, 20 U.S.C. § 1400 *et seq.*

Jacobs, H. H. (1997). *Mapping the big picture: Integrating curriculum and assessment K–12.* Alexandria, VA: Association for Supervision and Curriculum Development.

Jellison, J. A. (1979). The music therapist in the educational setting: Developing and implementing curriculum for the handicapped. *Journal of Music Therapy, 16,* 128–37.

Jellison, J. A. (1983). Functional value: A criterion for selection and prioritization of monmusic and music educational objectives in music therapy. *Music Therapy Perspectives, 1* (2), 17–22.

Jellison, J. A. (1999). Life beyond the jingle stick: Real music in a real world. *Update: Applications of Research in Music Education, 17* (2), 13–19.

Jellison, J. A. (2000). A content analysis of music research with children and youth with disabilities (1975–99): Applications in special education. In *Effectiveness of music therapy procedures: Documentation of research and clinical practice.* 3rd ed. (pp. 199–264). Silver Spring, MD: American Music Therapy Association.

Kagan, Spencer. (2000, July). *Structures for Standards.* Web site: www.kaganonline.com

Kansas State Department of Education. (1998). *Results-based staff development.* Topeka, KS: Author.

Little, J. W. (1982). Norms of collegiality and experimentation: Workplace conditions of school success. *American Educational Research Journal, 19,* 324–40.

Chapter 4
Communication: The Key to Effective Public Relations

A school is home to students, teachers, support staff, and administrators for most of the year, a complex community within the larger community. Traditionally, the life of a school has been rather insular; children attend classes, teachers do their jobs, and the day ends with little input from the parents or community at large. But this paradigm is rapidly changing as schools come under increasing scrutiny. Accountability issues have intensified the degree to which music supervisors must defend the value of arts programs in the school curriculum. With more resources being channeled to reading programs or mathematics courses, music supervisors and teachers spend more time advocating for music and the arts. It has become even more critical that the place of music and arts study in the educational system be understood, beyond the traditional attitude of "We've always had music programs, so they will certainly continue."

Systemic thinking, described by Peter Senge as the "fifth discipline" (1990), must be practiced by leaders in order to strengthen and galvanize the beliefs of the entire learning community: "Vision without systems thinking ends up painting lovely pictures of the future with no deep understanding of the forces that must be mastered to move from here to there" (p. 12). As music supervisors encounter challenges to their programs, they must be able to communicate the need for arts and music study as an integral part of a whole effort. Infused in the entire educational system, the arts provide safe and orderly learning opportunities for students to learn lifelong skills that promote self-awareness and self-discipline, offer differentiated approaches to instruction that can meet diverse learning-style needs, and give parents and members of the larger community the chance to participate in the life of the school. Music supervisors should be able to articulate the need for music and arts instruction in systemic terms and to arm their teachers with the necessary communication tools to argue for their programs with a holistic approach to advocacy.

The essence of good public relations depends upon sound, thoughtful, and respectful communication—and this is key to garnering support for and ensuring survival of music programs: working with a teacher struggling to meet the needs of her diverse student population; encouraging parents to become involved; creating "learning" statements to accompany artwork displays, music programs, or verbal announcements at concerts; quick, efficient customer service to the community—parents, teachers, and business leaders; and, most importantly, sharing a personal belief in and passion for music in the lives of children. "Communication, in all its forms, is the beginning, the middle, and the never-ending element of change. It's what makes things happen" (Kieffer, 2000, p. 21). Kieffer (2000) has collected a list of ten top drivers of successful communication taken from more than 20 case study presentations at a Clemson University conference on communications as a change accelerator:

1. "Know where you want to go: a clear destination point makes progress possible."
2. "Have people committed to leading the way: commitment powers progress."
3. "Be honest. You get to establish credibility once. You get to rebuild it forever."
4. "Be swift. You can't kill the rumor mill. The longer facts are delayed, the more the rumor mill will misconstrue them."
5. "Be accountable at every level. Make people responsible for their own change."
6. "Make communicating part of everyone's job." Put the tools in the hands of all teachers.
7. "Listen to people at all levels." Focus groups are faster than surveys.
8. "Give everyone a valued role and a chance to contribute."
9. "Walk the talk. If leadership expects different behavior, leadership must model different behavior."
10. "Keep repeating key messages. If it's important, repeat them until people recite them in their sleep" (p. 21).

All the music supervisors interviewed for this handbook placed emphasis on the importance of communication in promoting strong public relations as part of their jobs. Here are some samples of their comments:

- "To advocate is to exist!" (Don Doyle)
- Grant interviews to all media sources. If your district has a PR person, work closely with that person in your advocacy efforts.
- Highlight local and national programs in print.
- Serve on advisory boards or working committees for arts, business, community, and school-based organizations.
- "Know how to sit and talk." (Carol Crittenton)
- Actively educate your community.
- Be a model for what is good about the arts.
- Be an advocate for children.
- Be honest to everyone.

Dealing with Change through Public Relations

Today's schools have many more voices and diverse cultural backgrounds than ever before. In addition to adapting to rapidly changing demographics, schools must meet laws that require equal access for all students to educational opportunities. The immense possibilities of the Internet and other technologies also accentuate diversity and change. Because of this environment, Nemec (1999) writes, "There is more emphasis on strategic focus and a need to educate audiences. The creation of understanding and motivation, and eventually behavior changes, needs a more focused, people-to-people approach" (p. 27).

The music supervisor can help facilitate change in a school district or community by assuming the role of a "change agent." Agents of change move the process along. Gillis (1999), who writes that "organizations exist in two states: periods of change and periods of relative stability leading to change. Analyzed together, organizations are either preparing for change in an active mode or dealing with change in a reactive mode" (p. 28), describes three types of change agents that link to a three-phase cycle commonly experienced by organizations (see Figure 1. The Three Phase Cycle of Change). While music supervisors can serve as facilitators of change in a community, they must also be aware of myths and realities associated with effective communication (see Table 1. Myths and Realities of Effective Communication).

Leadership Skills in Public Relations

The Role of Facilitator

Supervisors commonly find themselves in the role of facilitators for both large and small groups. Though they have been taught to teach curricular content, help

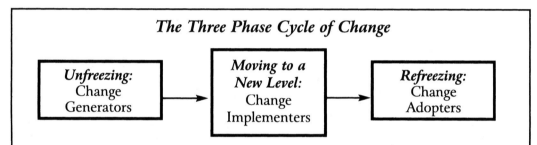

The Three Phase Cycle of Change

Unfreezing: Change Generators → **Moving to a New Level:** Change Implementers → **Refreezing:** Change Adopters

Unfreezing. A time when old habits are broken or old attitudes shaken. Change agents or "generators" in this stage are demonstrators, patrons, defenders, or leaders of change efforts. They are proactive in their leadership by continually alerting themselves and proposing solutions to emerging issues.

Moving to a New Level. A time of instability while new and old behaviors are in conflict. These change agents, or "change implementers," are members of the organizations who help move the change process along, deal with the resulting conflicts/stress associated with change, and help others focus on the future benefits that change can bring.

Refreezing. Consolidations of new behavior or attitude. "Change adopters" adopt current changes and model the new behavior or beliefs for others.

Note. The figure is based on Tamara Gillis, (April–May, 1999), "Change 101: Back to the Basics." *Communication World, 16* (3), 28.

Figure 1. The Three Phase Cycle of Change

Table 1. Myths and Realities of Effective Communication

Myth	Reality
More information is better.	Too much information is a major cause of stress and mistakes. Maintain clear and succinct information communication.
Engineer a message so that people will readily get it, diminishing what you may have had in mind originally.	Good communication works two ways. Allow others to add to, change, or embellish your message in their own way—get across the complete message through the most efficient means possible.
Districts should copy what other successful organizations do.	Every learning community is unique. Design messages that are distinctive to your system and image. Borrow ideas, but create your own design.
People appreciate slick presentations that obviously took a long time to prepare.	Most audiences want facts, not glitz. Current, credible information that is carefully crafted and presented will go much further.

Note. This table is modified from Diane Gayeski, (Oct.–Nov. 2000), "From Audits to Analytics," *Communication World, 17* (7), 30.

students learn information at hand, or prepare for concerts, their formal training as facilitators for adult groups is still not the norm. While some skills can be transferred from the classroom, working with adults is different in many ways. Because music supervisors lead meetings and working committees, effective facilitation skills are often learned in the saddle, by observing how people interact.

When working with people, dealing with conflict and the resolution of issues is a natural and common part of the process. Chapter 2 addressed the five conflict styles commonly found in groups who work or meet together and also discussed how the diverse learning styles can lead to conflict. With these styles in mind, the effective facilitator must set up meetings and working sessions that will accommodate various conflict and learning styles while accomplishing the goals of the work. Indeed, a better understanding of different conflict and learning styles can actually enhance a meeting or working session and is critical to the facilitator's success. Meeting participants can be assigned leadership roles that sometimes require them to move out of their personal styles and focus on their responsibilities during the session. Some of these roles may include the following:

The facilitator conducts the meeting for the purpose of planning, problem-solving, or achieving shared decisions. The facilitator's responsibilities extend to directing the meeting process, choreographing personalities and group energy, and maintaining focus by clarifying roles and processes, as well as ensuring that the agenda is clear and concise and that enough handouts are prepared. The facilitator should remain neutral.

The recorder supports in taking notes for the facilitator and comments by participants. The recorder keeps a record of the proceedings, using each participant's own language and asking the group for corrections, as well as inquiring what the group may consider inappropriate to record. The recorder may take public or regular minutes; when taking public minutes, the recorder prints with colored pens on chart paper on an easel to emphasize or highlight text, using upper- and lower-cased letters, bullets in front of phrases, and boxes for parts of the text. Public minutes can also be recorded effectively on computer with an LCD projector screen. The recorder also acts as a neutral participant.

The timekeeper works with the facilitator to determine an approximate amount of time for each agenda item. The timekeeper uses discretion to interrupt discussion so that participants are informed about the amount of time that has passed. Should the discussion warrant more time, the timekeeper must seek input from the facilitator and meeting participants regarding how long to extend the allotted time, so that either an effective conclusion is reached or a decision is made to place the matter on another meeting's agenda.

The task master is assigned when meetings may involve conflicting or difficult issues or personalities. While this might be the usual responsibility of the facilitator, in certain instances a task master is specifically charged with the duty of maintaining civility in group dynamics and keeping participants focused on the issues at hand. The task master is a neutral participant.

Building Consensus

Garmston and Wellman (1998) developed a very effective method for bringing groups to consensus. They advise that such conflict-promoting techniques as majority votes, averages, coin tosses, or bargaining should be avoided. In situations where a group with diverse opinions must come to a decision, Garmston and Wellman (1998) recommend the "Fist to Five" straw vote agreement method, in which the facilitator follows these steps: (1) Explain that the group should brainstorm solutions to the problem at hand, looking for the most acceptable alternative—not a win-lose result. Consensus does *not* mean a unanimous vote, everyone's first choice, or that everyone totally agrees with the final solution. (2) When the choices have been narrowed down, group votes are indicated by raising the number of fingers that indicate that participant's level of support: five fingers for "total agreement"; four for "agreement, support, good solution"; three for "willing to support"; two for "don't agree, will not support, will not sabotage"; one finger (or a fist) for "will openly resist." (3) With a two-fingers to a fist response, the person voting must communicate specific misgivings about the proposed solution. Discussion will be re-opened, and an alternative solution sought. Other straw votes are taken, until all group members agree to support the solution with three fingers. This method is especially effective for discussions regarding the particular wording of a document or the philosophical basis behind developing a document or changing a process.

Effective Meeting Agendas

Thoughtfully prepared agendas assist the facilitator to achieve the goals set forth by keeping the meeting focused and maintaining a reasonable length of time for each item listed. Agendas should be used in presentations, committee work, and meetings. The sample planner provided in Figure 2 includes questions that help facilitators create effective agendas.

Handling Hard Questions

The leader, facilitator, or presenter cannot expect to know the answer to everything. The best advice for handling difficult questions is to pause, take a deep breath, think, and then respond, preferably in that order. If unsure, do not guess. Several techniques help with answering such questions, including restating the question, repackaging the question, or referring the question to someone else. In each case, restating the question in your own words helps to clarify the question's intent and content and

---

Agenda Planner

What is the purpose of this meeting or work session?

What do we need to accomplish—in specific terms?

What issues or challenges do we face?

Who will attend this meeting?

What roles should I assign to which participants?

For the facilitator's use

Meeting logistics
Date: _____
Time: _____
Location: _____

Person responsible for arrangements: _____
    Contact Information: _____

Figure 2. Agenda Planner

helps the respondent to more clearly prepare a response. At times, questions may be stated in a hostile or negative manner. To "repackage" such questions allows the respondent to diffuse the confrontation and present the matter in a more positive light.

Selling Ideas

"We are in the business of sell!" reports Carol Crittendon, a music supervisor who was surveyed for this book. As a supervisor, selling ideas is a part of providing vision. After solidifying a vision or idea, begin "planting seeds" with stakeholders who will be involved. Often, new ideas mean change, and change takes time. Avoiding surprises by discussing ideas helps to establish support and provide important feedback that can further shape how the ideas will be accepted by others. When the time comes to make presentations about the ideas, practice out loud and mentally see yourself speaking to others. Use visuals to illustrate points; always ask for input from your audience. Make clear, concise recommendations as part of the presentation, including benefits, potential concerns, and costs. Finally, ask for listeners' support and pursue a time for follow-up.

Advocacy Resources

Many resources assist with the promotion of music education. MENC's Web site (www.menc.org) offers many links to advocacy sites. The American Music Conference (AMC) has developed a Web-based version of the Music Education Advocate's Toolkit produced by NAMM-The International Music Products Association (www.amc-music.org). The physical toolkit contains these materials on CD-ROM, along with many other offerings (it can be purchased through MENC at 800-828-0229). The Web-based version includes sample letters, press releases, and research summaries (www.namm.com).

Several of the arts education organizations listed in Chapter 3 also have pertinent advocacy resources. In particular, the Arts Education Partnership (aep-arts.org) has an on-line version of the document *Champions of Change: Involvement in the Arts and Human Development.* This important document includes results from Catterall's analysis (1999) of the Department of Education's NESL:88 study that implies that music learning has positive effects on mathematics and other academic and social skills.

Effective Presentations

In *The Turbo Team Training Kit,* Larry Holpp (1999) lists eight secrets for effective public speaking: (1) start in quickly by introducing a motivating factor such as posing a question, promising a result, or insinuating some benefit; (2) keep the topic disciplined to a limited number of clear ideas, underpropped with conclusions and suggested results; keep ideas connected; (3) be visually demonstrative, both in words and actual images; (4) direct the message to the needs of the audience—do whatever advance work is necessary to not only know and affirm their needs but to be ready to receive their reactions; (5) challenge the audience to concrete efforts and be the first to take on the challenge; (6) build upon factual and emotional arguments; use facts to buttress feelings with an appeal that is not limited to factual arguments; (7) be sparing with humor that is tasteful, serves the arguments, and does not have the potential to offend any members of the audience; (8) keep the audience focused and affirmed by restating and summarizing ideas and relating them to actions (pp. 2–9).

Recommended Web Sites

The Internet provides enormous potential for communication. Most school districts now have their own Web sites that include calendars, personnel contact information, position openings, and highlights of the educational environment. But, as technology advances and Web sites become more sophisticated, user expectations include a certain appearance quality and tools for easy searching and browsing. The following list includes one book and several sites that, though they may become obsolescent as quickly as hard-copy books in this day of rapidly changing technology, provide excellent Web site layout and design information:

- **CAST Bobby** (www.cast.org/bobby/), a free service provided by CAST, helps Web-page authors identify and repair significant barriers to access by individuals with disabilities.
- **Skyways** (//skyways.lib.ks.us/towns/lessons/tools.htm) gives helpful tools for building Web pages.
- **Meta Builder 2** (//vancouver-webpages.com/META/mk-metas.html) helps generate HTML META tags.
- **A Dictionary of HTML META tags** (vancouver-webpages.com/META/) provides tags that allow better indexing by robot-driven search engines, such as AltaVista (www.altavista.digital.com), Infoseek (//infoseek.go.com), and searchBC (//vancouver-webpages.com/searchBC.html).
- **RGB Color Charts** (www.hypersolutions.org/rgb.html) provides color charts that contain an approximation (the numbers are exact; the colors as close as technology can get them) of a color palette that is Web browser safe.
- **W3C HTML Validation Service** (//validator.w3.org/) checks HTML documents for conformance to W3C HTML and XHTML Recommendations and other HTML standards.
- Krug, Steve. (2000). *Don't make me think! A common sense approach to Web usability.* Indianapolis, IN: QUE (Macmillan).

Public Relations: Parting Suggestions

These tips on effective interaction encourage the kind of poise that makes for good public relations work under any circumstance:
- Continually work to improve effective communication skills. Communication is at the heart of every leadership responsibility.
- Mentally construct the setting and situation before presenting ideas, facilitating a meeting, or speaking to a large audience.

- Anticipate questions in advance and internalize your responses before going public.
- Give written communication time to settle. If possible, write the letter, article, or position on one day and revisit it on another day before submitting it.
- Respect the opinions of others, whether you agree or disagree. Almost all behaviors are motivated by positive intention or opinion.

References

Catterall, James S., Chapleau, Richard, and Iwanga, John. (1999). Involvement in the arts and human development: General involvement and intensive involvement in music and theater arts. *Champions of change: The impact of the arts on learning.* Washington, DC: Arts Education Partnership.

Garmston, Robert, and Wellman, Bruce. (1998). *The adaptive school: Developing and facilitating collaborative groups,* 3rd ed. El Dorato Hills, CA: Four Hats Seminars.

Gayeski, Diane. (Oct.–Nov. 2000). From audits to analytics. *Communication World, 17* (7), 28–31.

Gillis, Tamara. (April–May 1999). Change 101. Back to the basics. *Communication World, 16* (3), 28–29.

Holpp, L. (1999). *The team turbo training kit.* New York: McGraw-Hill.

Kieffer, Dave. (Oct.–Nov. 2000). Tricks of the trade. *Communication World, 17* (7), 21.

Nemec, Richard. (Feb.–March 1999). PR or advertising: Who's on top? *Communication World, 16* (3), 25–28.

Senge, Peter. (1990). *The fifth discipline: The art and practice of the learning organization.* New York: Currency Doubleday.

Chapter 5
Recruiting, Hiring, and Evaluating

The U.S. teacher shortage becomes more serious every year. According to Recruiting New Teachers, Inc. (2000), the following statistics give great cause for concern:

- In the next ten years, America will need to hire two million teachers. Half of the current teachers will retire, and enrollment will increase by three million.
- All of the nation's major urban school districts have an urgent need for teachers in at least one of the high-need subject areas, such as special education (97.5%), science (97.5%), or math (95%).
- Urban districts will need to hire 700,000 new teachers in the coming decade.
- More than half of the districts (52.5%) need more elementary teachers and more male teachers (82.5%).

In addition, Linda Darling-Hammond (2001) has reported that

> The number of new teachers currently prepared each year—roughly 190,000—is more than enough to satisfy the demand. However, there is a shortage of candidates who are willing to work under the work and salary conditions in specific locations. Therefore, although some states and districts are experiencing shortfalls, others have surpluses. (p. 12)

With this overwhelming demand, human resource offices, as well as district curriculum specialists (including music supervisors) are working to devise attractive lures for teachers in order to fill openings. These lures include creating engaging sites on the World Wide Web, moving up hiring dates to get their pick of candidates, offering generous signing bonuses, loan-forgiveness plans, mentoring programs, health-club memberships, and the promise of mortgage supplements (Johnson, 2000). Susan Johnson (2000) a professor at Harvard University, has researched the next generation of teachers and found that "as a group they value job security, prefer autonomy to teamwork, tolerate isolation, eschew competition, respect authority, disavow the importance of pay, oppose differential treatment within their ranks, and express little interest in career advancement" (p. 48).

Johnson (2000) describes what public education should do to attract this new generation of teachers:

1. Establish various pathways to teaching. Part of the current shortage dilemma is the fact that those who would like to explore teaching as a profession are leery of making a long-term commitment to the profession, particularly when the pay is so low. Teacher education programs with lengthy and expensive requirements prevent some people with expertise in a field—but no teaching credentials—from investigating teaching as a profession. However, schools that find they need to hire teachers with only provisional licenses must, therefore, work to ensure these teachers' future conviction to the profession. Across the country, states and local school districts are beginning to create alternate routes to certification. "What most of these programs have in common is the requirement that a candidate possess a bachelor's degree, pass a competency examination and a background check, and complete a compressed training program that includes intensive, hands-on experience. After initial training, the new teacher usually receives support from a mentor teacher or supervisor" (Finn and Madigan, 2001, p. 31). Berry (2001) warns that alternative programs can potentially be simply a quick fix (p. 33). And, in New York, 15 percent of the alternative recruits quit just two months into the school year. Berry (2001) suggests some high-quality routes to alternative certification that include:

- providing strong academic and pedagogical coursework so that students can reach the state's curriculum standards
- offering intensive field experience in the form of internships or student-teaching
- assuring that alternative candidates meet all the state's standards for subject matter and teaching knowledge
- guaranteeing that new teachers pass the same assessments given to their traditionally prepared counterparts (p. 35).

2. Organize schools to promote teamwork. While the new generation mirrors the attitudes of previous generations in desiring autonomy in their work, successful models in business and education point to the need to assist, encourage, and critique each other's efforts. Mentoring, release time to observe skilled colleagues, curriculums that serve as guidance about what and how to teach, and peers and administrators who offer positive suggestions and assessments on teaching performance are a few of the ways this can happen. David Berliner (2000) adds, "Mentoring programs cut the dropout rate of teachers from roughly 50 to 15 percent during the first five years of teaching. Mentoring is very important; without it, our shortages will grow" (p. 10).

3. Encourage teachers to assume varied responsibilities. Offering opportunities to lead and influence learning environments broadens a teacher's depth of understanding and skills. Early on, the teacher might be asked to pilot a new curriculum, team teach, organize a teacher study group, write a grant, or serve on the school's site council. Allowing for varied experiences enriches the teacher's perspectives about the world outside the classroom.

4. Offer differentiated pay for teachers who assume additional responsibilities. A study in *Education Week* (Johnson, 2000) reveals that teachers aged 22 to 28 earn $8,000 less than other college-educated peers. By the time teachers have reached 44 years of age, they earn $32,511 less than peers with a master's degree. The new generation of teachers appears more willing to explore alternative approaches to compensation and believes that performance and value should influence salary.

5. Teachers' unions should provide progressive leadership to change the current system. Johnson's research (2000) demonstrates that the new generation of teachers is more likely to be attracted by progressive unions, peer reviews, differentiated pay, and less regulation at the school site.

In her report "Solving the Dilemmas of Teacher Supply, Demand, and Standards: How We Can Ensure a Competent, Caring, and Qualified Teacher for Every Child," Linda Darling-Hammond (2000) summarizes various reasons why schools have difficulty filling shortages. In some states, such as California and Nevada, finding teachers is problematic because the state prepares relatively few teachers but has a rapidly growing student enrollment. Some states and districts appear to create their own shortage by imposing a complicated, lengthy hiring process. Before it was overhauled, Fairfax County in Virginia imposed a 62-step hiring process that often discouraged teachers from applying. Teachers who are fully credentialed and experienced in one state are discouraged by some states' lack of license reciprocity, which sometimes forces them to complete difficult or redundant requirements—such as passing a state's basic skills test. Other barriers include a lack of pension portability across states, loss of salary credit for teachers who move, and the tendency of some districts to push hiring decisions to August or September.

Darling-Hammond's report (2000) also describes policies that have worked to ensure highly qualified teachers in exemplary states and districts, as well as to boost student achievement. Her suggestions for policy reforms include the following: (1) link teacher standards with salaries; (2) create service scholarship programs to prepare high-ability candidates in shortage fields; (3) establish licensing reciprocity across states; (4) create national recruitment initiatives, streamline hiring procedures, and develop on-line information technologies; (5) expand teacher education programs in high-need fields; (6) provide incentives for more extended (five-year and fifth-year) teacher education programs; (7) provide incentives for college pathways that prepare paraprofessionals for certification; (8) create high-quality induction programs; and (9) "Just say no" to hiring unqualified teachers (Darling-Hammond, 2000, pp. 15–17).

Leadership Roles in Recruiting and Hiring

All the supervisors interviewed for this handbook are involved with the recruiting and hiring practices of their districts. While, in many cases, recruiting efforts are mainly undertaken by the personnel or human resources staff in the district, music supervisors play an important role in finalizing the hire. For instance, several supervisors are responsible for hiring itinerant teachers, such as orchestra or band directors who travel from building to building. Supervisors also assist building principals with the final cut of applicants in teacher selection, helping to match personalities and instructional goals. In all cases, supervisors advise others to maintain a close relationship with human resources staff and building principals in order to acquire the best candidates.

Norris and Richburg (1997) suggest some strategies for selecting top teachers:

1. *"Start early."* Don't wait until resignations are final to begin looking to fill

vacancies in the next school year; if necessary, begin in September of the prior year to collect a pool of candidates.

2. *"Develop attractive recruiting materials."* The cash outlay for an attractive, full-color brochure that includes colorful evidence of the quality of life in the school community is a great investment. In addition, the school district Web site should expand on the brochure and provide links to places of interest, descriptions of school district and community events, personnel, job openings for both classified and unclassified personnel, and school/community goals. The Web site can be regularly updated and should exude enthusiasm about the quality of the educational program.

3. *"Build a strong candidate pool."* Seek out good candidates by visiting face-to-face with key faculty members in the education departments of selected universities. Instructors are anxious for their strongest students to be hired. Additionally, observe perspective candidates as they student teach—establishing an early relationship with student teachers helps them feel wanted and respected by your district before they send out applications to other districts. Career fairs are an important effort as well, and occasionally experienced teachers will also attend.

4. *"Announce your vacancies."* On your state map, locate all of the colleges with education departments in a chosen area (Norris and Richburg suggest a 200-mile radius) and do a mailing that includes vacant position announcements, name and location of your district, deadline for applications, the name of a contact person, and a request for a formal letter of application stating specific reasons for the applicant's interest in applying for the position.

5. *"Form a hiring committee."* Hiring committees should consist of administrators, district staff, and veteran teachers. Depending on the size of the district, four to six people are normally on the interview committee. The new hire could potentially be mentored by the veteran teacher who participated in the interview.

6. *"Screen applicants."* The application that a potential candidate fills out can reveal very little or a great deal about that person. Many applications are screened for spelling, punctuation, English usage, and neatness. Even grade point averages are important but may not reveal much about the candidate's true abilities. Including other questions—such as "college activities"—can flag a candidate's interest in working with and helping others. Music students have many opportunities to participate in performance ensembles in and out of school, work with children in a variety of settings, and expand their base of experiences through travel and community work. In addition, asking candidates to write a paragraph about a carefully selected topic reveals a great deal about the applicant's knowledge and breadth of experience.

7. *"Interview candidates."* Many school districts have found that structured interviews allow candidates to describe what they would do or how they would feel in certain circumstances. Interviews should always be at least an hour, and the interview committee should not comment about the candidates they have interviewed until the session is complete. The interview committee should remember that they, too, must maintain eye contact, smile, and react positively to the comments of each candidate.

8. *"Observe the candidate in action."* In some cases, it may be necessary to invite final-ists to the school for a teaching demonstration. Candidates must be given specific infor-mation about the subject and the class they will be asked to teach. No guidelines should be given about how the candidates should teach; only the content is provided. Members of the hiring committee should come to a consensus on the specific skills or attributes that they are looking for, including the ability to interact with children effectively.

9. *"Award the contract."* Deciding about first and alternative candidates by mid-April reduces the chance that they will be hired by another district. It is also very important to prepare a biographical summary of new faculty members for the board of directors so that they are made aware of the thoroughness of your search and the quality of the hire. Be sure to praise the time and efforts of the hiring committee publicly.

10. *"Follow-up."* Try to assign the new teacher—whether experienced or new to the profession—a mentor. Civic groups, teacher organizations, and building admin-istrators can help new teachers feel welcomed and honored in the community by hosting picnics, luncheons, or other welcoming events. Allow the mentoring teacher and the new teacher time to visit each other's classrooms (p. 46).

A recent study (Farkas, Johnson, & Foleno, 2000) found that, overall, school admin-istrators find the quality of new teachers either "improved (52%) or stayed the same (39%). Asked whether the supply or the quality of teachers is more problematic, 50% of administrators point to quantity, one-third (32%) point to quality, and another 13% volunteer that neither is a problem." In other words, the encouraging news about today's teachers is that they are, in the eyes of administrators, better prepared than ever.

MENC (2000) has produced a useful brochure entitled *Promoting the Profession: Recruiting and Retaining Music Teachers,* which has many helpful suggestions for state music education associations and local school districts. The U.S. Department of Education has created the *Survival Guide for New Teachers* (DePaul, 2000), based on interviews with winners of the Sallie Mae First Class Teacher Awards for outstand-ing elementary and secondary performance during their first year of teaching. Tips for first-year teachers include working with veteran teachers, parents, and college and university professors and building a relationship with principals. Related infor-mation, including Web sites, is also provided.

Licensure

Several licensing and certification organizations exist whose purposes are to establish high standards regarding what teachers should know and be able to do and to advance related education reforms. As mentoring practices between the school, post-secondary institution, the new teacher, and the mentoring teacher are expanded across the nation, K–12 schools will become deeply involved in teacher licensing. Teacher preparation will include three phases: (1) preservice preparation, in which the preservice teacher must meet national standards developed and applied by members of the teaching profession and public; (2) extended clinical preparation and assessment, including a provisional license granted after completion of a teacher-education program, with a more permanent license granted by the state after the teacher has one or more years of experience in the classroom and meets the state's requirements for that license; and (3) continuing professional development, whereby school districts and state agencies require teachers to continue professional development to maintain their licenses or move higher on the salary scales.

The following licensing organizations along with state department of education licensing processes are responsible for assuring a comprehensive system for teacher preparation. Music supervisors need to be aware of these organizations, particularly when, as a nation, we are working to meet teacher shortages and improve teacher quality. Quality assurance in teacher education, when viewed through the metaphor of a three-legged stool (NCATE, INTASC, NBPTS), enables schools and colleges of education to be guided by professional standards:

The National Council for Accreditation of Teacher Education (NCATE), recognized by the U.S. Department of Education as the accrediting body for colleges and universities that prepare teachers and other professional personnel for work in elementary and secondary schools, has published *Standards, Procedures, and Policies for the Accreditation of Professional Education Units* (1997). Through its voluntary, peer-review process, NCATE ensures that accredited institutions produce competent, caring, and qualified teachers and other school personnel who can help all students learn. NCATE, a nonprofit, nongovernmental organization, is a coalition of more than thirty national associations representing the education profession at large. The associations that comprise NCATE appoint representatives to NCATE's policy boards, which develop NCATE standards, policies, and procedures. Membership on policy boards includes representatives from organizations of teacher educators, teachers, state and local policy makers, and professional specialists (for more information, see the NCATE Web site at www.ncate.org).

The National Board for Professional Teaching Standards (NBPTS) is a national certification board that certifies experienced teachers who have demonstrated accomplished practice in their own classrooms; the NBPTS publication is entitled *What Teachers Should Know and Be Able to Do* (1994). This board was established in response to the Carnegie Task Force on Teaching as a Profession publication *A Nation Prepared: Teachers for the Twenty-First Century* (1986). NBPTS has certified nearly 10,000 teachers and expects to certify more than 100,000 by 2006. Teachers who receive this certification now receive financial incentives including fee reimbursements and salary supplements in forty states. Teachers are required to develop strenuous portfolio documentation of their instruction that includes intensive reflection and analysis (for more information, see the NBPTS Web site at www.nbpts.org).

The Interstate New Teacher Assessment and Support Consortium (INTASC), a program of the Council of Chief State School Officers, has crafted standards for licensing new teachers entitled *Model Standards for Beginning Teacher Licensing and Development: A Resource for State Dialogue* (1992). As a result, performance assessment learning outcomes as outlined by INTASC serve as the means by which a unit is able to show how its outcomes are contributing to the achievement of state standards. The mission of INTASC is to promote standards-based reform of teacher preparation, licensing, and professional development. To carry out this mission, INTASC provides a vehicle for states to work jointly on formulating model policy to reform teacher preparation and licensing and instruments to assess the classroom performance of a teacher (for more information, see the INTASC Web site at www.ccsso.org/intasc.html).

National Association of Schools of Music (NASM) was founded in 1924 to secure a better understanding among institutions of higher education engaged in work in music; to establish a more uniform method of granting credit; and to develop and maintain basic, threshold standards for the granting of degrees and other credentials. NASM fulfills these purposes, aims, and objectives by acting as a specialized, professional accrediting agency; by providing counsel and assistance to established and developing institutions and programs; by publishing information about professional development and holding annual meetings and other forums; by pursuing analysis and policy studies on issues in music, the arts, education, accreditation, and cultural development; and by providing information to the general public about accreditation and its relationship to educational programs in music.

Evaluating Teachers: Developing Personal and Program Goals

In many cases, music supervisors have some responsibilities for the evaluation of district teachers. An excellent resource for supervisors is David P. Doerksen's MENC publication, *Guide to Evaluating Teachers of Music Performance Groups* (1990). Doerksen gives nuts-and-bolts information about the evaluation process, job descriptions, model forms, and an excellent bibliography. Most teacher evaluations include the following general performance criteria:

Professional and personal: skill of pedagogy (teaching methods), appropriateness of content, clear communication, positive attitudes, and adherence to professional behavior and district policies

Planning: appropriateness of lesson plans and units for the student population and clear, sequentially delivered objectives aligned with curriculum

Classroom or activity management: orderly, supportive learning environment; appropriate disciplinary actions or prevention; adherence to building/district policy

Teaching ability: selection of appropriate amount of time to deliver depth of content; well-paced, engaging delivery; and use of a variety of instructional strategies based on principles of learning

Evaluation: effective and appropriate evaluation and assessments of student learning; fairness and consistency; and well-communicated grading system and prompt feedback.

For new teachers, classroom management is the most challenging area of their development. While many teachers are reasonably effective in managing behavior, a few may need intensive assistance. The majority can improve their practices with a modest amount of help. Direct intervention by building-level administrators and mentoring or peer assistance by fellow teachers are the most effective means of helping their improvement. MENC has recently published *Classroom Management in General, Choral, and Instrumental Music Programs* (Moore, Batey, & Royse, 2002), which cites many sources for classroom behavior and management.

Peer Coaching (Mentoring)

Both new and experienced teachers have found that the practice of mentoring is worthwhile for professional development. Studies conducted by Scott (1999) in New Brunswick, Canada, found that 96% of new teachers and 98% of experienced teachers benefited from the mentoring process. Comprehensive and well-designed mentoring programs have lowered the attrition rates of new teachers (National Association of State Boards of Education, 1998). However, simply having a mentor is not effective; a formal, comprehensive program that provides mentor teachers with specific knowledge and skills related to their new and expanded role of providing guidance and support is necessary. Holloway (2001) describes the California Formative Assessment and Support System for Teachers (CFASST) as a collaborative system designed for beginning teachers and mentors: "Trained mentors help novice teachers plan lessons, assist them in gathering information about best practices, observe the new teachers' classes, and provide feedback. The novice teachers reflect on their practice and apply what they have learned to future lessons" (p. 85).

When music teacher mentors work with new teachers, the mentor's mode of operation should be established at the beginning of the relationship. The mentor's working modes might include the establishment of the following:

- mentoring criteria for the learner (usually a new teacher): mutually develop goals for each session, coach with sensitivity to the learner, seek the learner's desire to learn and improve performance, and encourage ideas and suggestions.
- ways to communicate effective teaching practices: work from simple to complex, verbally review the desired performance using appropriate examples, role-play situations, model the lesson or how to handle a situation, and have the learner describe the instruction to the mentor.
- positive working relationships: confirm the learner's potential, share stories about personal experiences with the new teacher, seek out the learner's concerns and perceptions, allow for safe risk-taking, and communicate high expectations for the learner.
- mentor observation procedures: videotape the learner's teaching performance in order to discuss specific behaviors later, maintain a low profile, avoid interference with the learner's teaching through body language or inappropriate words, and solicit any last minute concerns or questions from the learner before the teaching session.
- a system for follow-up: praise the learner's efforts; provide timely, detailed feedback; seek assurance that the learner will continue to practice teaching skills; schedule additional coaching sessions; and seek feedback about mentoring effectiveness from the learner.

Working with Difficult Situations

Despite every effort, supervisors sometimes encounter difficult situations in evaluating teachers, supervising mentoring programs, or dealing with colleagues or the public. Holpp (1999) lists the following guidelines for dealing directly with difficult situations:

- Make statements that are specific and address behaviors: Use examples when describing the problem and its consequences; focus on the issue and not the person (avoid personal attacks).
- Summarize the effects that the situation has created: Explain how the problem affects students; focus on the details of the problem and avoid feelings and emotions.
- Be attentive to the other person's perspective: Understand the other person's perception and history of the problem by seeking his or her input for ideas and solutions before expressing your own; identify and clarify any source of resistance from the other person; and always ask, "What else can you tell me?"
- Develop a shared understanding: Help the other person brainstorm with you on some ideas for alternative action or behavior, propose a mutually established solution that establishes common ground between you, and create follow-up plans for implementing solutions (pp. 2–7).

Parting Staffing Suggestions

With these guidelines in mind, supervisors can be more fully prepared to face the various challenges of recruiting, hiring, and evaluating teachers:

- Be aware of and be involved in recruiting and hiring practices in your district.
- Learn about the various programs for licensing teachers and accrediting schools.
- Advocate for effective teacher training for both preservice and in-service professional development.
- Study models of classroom- and behavior-management to determine what will work most efficiently for your district and community.
- Encourage mentoring and peer coaching with the music staff.
- Work with building and district administration to establish effective criteria for mentoring programs.
- Focus on issues and not personal agendas when dealing with difficult situations.

References

Berliner, David. (2000). Improving the quality of the teaching force. *Educational Leadership, 58* (8), 10.

Berry, Barnett. (2001). No shortcuts to preparing good teachers. *Educational Leadership, 58* (8), 33–35.

Carnegie Task Force on Teaching as a Profession. (1986). *A nation prepared: Teachers for the twenty-first century.* New York: Author.

Darling-Hammond, Linda. (2000). *Solving the dilemmas of teacher supply, demand, and standards: How we can ensure a competent, caring, and qualified teacher for every child.*

New York: National Commission on Teaching & America's Future. (Web site: www.tc.edu/nctaf/)

Darling-Hammond, Linda. (2001). The challenges of staffing our schools. *Educational Leadership, 58* (8), 12.

DePaul, Amy. (2000). *Survival guide for new teachers: How new teachers can work effectively with veteran teachers, parents, principals, and teacher educators.* Washington, DC: U.S. Department of Education Office of Educational Research and Improvement.

Doerksen, David P. (1990). *Guide to evaluating teachers of music performance groups.* Reston, VA: MENC.

Farkas, S., Johnson, J., & Foleno, T. (2000). *A sense of calling: Who teaches and why.* New York: Public Agenda.

Finn, Chester E., Jr., & Madigan, Kathleen. (2001). Removing the barriers for teacher candidates. *Educational Leadership, 58* (8), 31.

Holloway, John H. (2001). The benefits of mentoring. *Educational Leadership, 58* (8), 85.

Holpp, Larry. (1999). *The team turbo training kit.* New York: McGraw-Hill.

Interstate New Teacher Assessment and Support Consortium. (1992). *Model standards for beginning teacher licensing and development: A resource for state dialogue.* Washington, DC: Council of Chief State School Officers.

Johnson, Susan Moore. (2000). Teaching's next generation. *Education Week, 6* (7), 48.

MENC. (2000). *Promoting the profession: Recruiting and retaining music teachers.* Reston, VA: Author.

National Association of State Boards of Education. (1998). *The numbers game.* Alexandria, VA: Author.

National Board for Professional Teaching Standards. (1994). *What teachers should know and be able to do.* Southfield, MI: Author.

National Council for the Accreditation of Teacher Education. (1997). *Standards, procedures, and policies for the accreditation of professional education units.* Washington, DC: Author.

Moore, M. C., Batey, A. L., & Royse, D. M. (2002). *Classroom management in general, choral, and instrumental music programs.* Reston, VA: MENC.

Norris, Gary, and Richburg, Robert. (1997). Hiring the best. *The American School Board Journal, 184* (11), 46–48, 55.

Recruiting New Teachers, Inc. (2000). *Field facts: Urban teacher challenge report,* p. 1. (Web site: www.rnt.org/facts/facts.html, May 7, 2000)

Scott, N. H. (1999). *Supporting new teachers: A report on the 1998–99 beginning teacher induction program in New Brunswick, Canada.* (Eric Document Reproduction Services No. ED 437347).

Chapter 6
Finance

Music supervisors entering the twenty-first century have found that, rather than acquiring funding for their programs through local sources, most of the general funds available for schools come from the state level, as a result of state taxes. Federal funding for music programs is rare. Usually, more than half of a state's federal funds are used for food services, followed by entitlement programs such as Title I, Special Education, and Carl Perkins. With state monies, however, come additional demands for accountability. The supervisor is, therefore, advised to pay close attention to discussion, laws, and initiatives from the state or federal levels that may affect funding for their programs.

Max Kirst (1986) describes the complex political and dynamic interrelationships surrounding school financing: "Public school policymaking is embedded in a complex social matrix. It is not possible to consider the future of U.S. schools without examining the size and distribution of future populations, the future state of the economy and its effect on funds available for the schools, and the political context within which decisions will be made. The public school system is a 'dependent variable' of larger social and economic forces" (p. 341). Current funding trends are beginning to link schools' "productivity" with the potential amount of capital received. Often "productivity" is the practice of holding schools accountable solely on the basis of assessment scores on math and reading skills. Richard Rothstein (2000) of the Economic Policy Institute points out that while we are quick to measure school output by math and reading scores, "We require schools to produce a much broader range of outcomes, most of which are unmeasured and some of which are unmeasurable" (p. 11). Rothstein argues that longitudinal data for math and reading performance claiming to show declining productivity is poorly measured and reported. "Then and now" comparisons (current reading abilities versus those abilities of children long ago) cannot be taken seriously because of dramatic demographic changes and lack of information about parental education, occupation, family income, race, ethnicity, and other socioeconomic characteristics that were not factored "then."

Additionally, little energy is devoted to measuring many other important school outputs. "Not only do we have no standardized reports of adolescents' physical health, but we have no (or very limited) trend data on the national goals of responsible citizenship; avoidance of drug, alcohol, and tobacco abuse; competency in fields like the arts; knowledge about the diverse heritage of this nation and the world community; or participation in community service and activities demonstrating personal responsibility" (Rothstein, 2000, p. 13).

Music supervisors must be vigilant about informing the school and community about the "outputs" of district music programs. While arts programs are rarely considered a part of the accountability system, the public must be made constantly aware of the benefits of music and arts education in terms of productivity issues.

Dealing with Funding Formulas

School funding formulas are usually determined by the state's supreme court. Because of the varying levels of wealth from district to district, equity issues are prevalent, and formulas are often challenged. The foremost issue for superintendents and financial administrators is the allocation of district teacher salaries. Salary negotiations both at the state and district levels are significant events, of which supervisors should be keenly aware. Usually the state teacher's union provides information received from the state regarding the availability of funds for a given year. With that information, the district determines how much will be spent on salaries and then on the allocation for everything else.

Music supervisors can provide leadership to assure that sufficient money is set aside for their programs. Most work closely to maintain effective communication with district-office financial officers, including establishing a good track record for managing funds for arts programs. Many of the supervisors surveyed indicated that even in tough financial times, money could be found to operate programs if working relationships were strong. The supervisor should be sensitive to the parameters of how much to ask for and should balance that with the needs of the entire district. The supervisor should also establish strong priorities for the distribution of funds. Turning in reports completed and on time and maintaining consistent communication enhances the supervisor's relationship with the financial officer.

Funding Procedures for Music Supervisors

Contract Negotiations

Supervisors should quickly become familiar with negotiation practices in their state. Negotiations for teacher contracts are carried out in most states on a district-by-district basis. Items like planning time are called "mandatory negotiable" items by law because they deal with amounts and conditions of work. Evening and weekend work is often addressed under a job description or as part of the supplemental salary schedule. Teacher/pupil ratios are sometimes negotiated both at the state and local levels.

In negotiation processes, it is important for supervisors to be aware of which side of the negotiations they represent. For instance, if they represent teachers, they need to approach the teachers' negotiating team about a proposal. If they represent the Board of Education (as an administrator), they need to take their proposals to the Board's negotiating team.

Budget Categories

All district music supervisors interviewed indicated that they were responsible for overseeing the distribution of capital outlay and general fund dollars for the teachers they represent. Every district has its own procedures, and the supervisor must quickly become familiar with them. Normally, purchase authorizations for instruments, equipment, and texts are monitored by the central office. The supervisor is given a budget limit and timelines in which spending must occur. In larger districts, a faculty member becomes chair for the music teaching area with the task of accumulating the needs of all the music teachers and turning in budget requests to the central office. In small districts, the supervisor may be responsible for all school music budget needs.

Budget categories are usually divided into several subcategories: supplies (for offices, studios, and classrooms), equipment (musical instruments, office equipment, music stands, classroom instruments, and computers), textbooks and supplementary book materials, pianos (sometimes part of the equipment budget), and maintenance (piano tuning, repairs, etc.).

Equipment Purchases

Local boards of education generally set a maximum figure for the purchase of equipment without the submission of formal bids. Purchases made below this figure present few problems. However, if it is necessary for bids to be submitted, the variance in quality of construction and manufacture may be so great that it may be virtually impossible to assure a school system or music school of appropriate equipment—unless a specific, uniform program is established. A supervisor must establish a consistent educational philosophy regarding instrument purchases. Is the lowest bid the best bid, given the longevity, quality, and tonal satisfaction of an instrument? Cowden and Klotman (1991) recommend three categories of instrument specifications: (1) *first-line instruments*—highest quality construction and tone; (2) *second-line instruments*—acceptable tone, and average life; and (3) *third-line instruments*—low-quality tone and construction (p.163). When selecting a standard for purchase, be certain that all dealers are bidding on the same level of instrument quality. Obviously, low-quality instruments will bring a lower bid than high-quality instruments, but the trade-off for poor construction and tone may not be in the best interest of the music program. Instrument agreement and repair forms are found in Appendix F.

Maintenance

The supervisors surveyed had the following suggestions concerning maintenance:
- Inspect and tune pianos on a regular schedule; this prolongs the life of the instruments and promotes good musical ears.
- Audition and interview piano tuners and place them under contract or written agreement.
- If your district has an in-house repair shop, set up procedures for each school to supervise its own instrument maintenance.

- Establish repair procedures that don't interfere with students' rehearsals.
- Pre-establish specifications and costs for maintenance and repairs.
- Keep bows, mouthpieces, strings, pads, and so forth on hand to avoid lost instructional time.
- Be aware of insurance policies for your district.

Music and Text Selection

Procedures for music and text selection vary from district to district. Common approaches have teachers field-test texts being considered for adoption. In Lincoln, Nebraska, public schools, the teachers doing the field-testing also meet with publisher representatives. These teachers are surveyed (see Appendix E) and their recommendations presented to all teachers in the district. The books are examined for reading level, affirmative action concerns, and alignment to district/state curriculum. Most texts are generally rotated every 5 to 10 years.

In the Olathe, Kansas, schools, textbook revisions are part of the five-year curriculum revision cycle. In the first year of the cycle, teachers revisit and update existing curriculum. In year two, teachers look at textbook resources that match criteria they have determined necessary to help support their new curriculum. These criteria may include readability, illustrations, content, and philosophical base. The committee engages in a "blind" text search, placing the agreed-upon criteria before the name of the publisher. Sections of the books are copied without the book title on various paper colors. Teachers pilot the colored book selections in class, discuss pros and cons with their peers, and vote by color on which selections best match their criteria. At the secondary level, one of the criteria for purchase is "How many classes will the book serve?" When finances are tight, this criterion is critical in establishing priorities for purchases. The number of texts ordered can be phased in through the cycle so that the capital outlay can be spread over time.

Music, on the other hand, is selected each year. Larger communities or towns with active music stores often offer yearly music-reading clinics. Large groups of music teachers gather to sing or play through the newest selections. Often, some music for contests is selected from these reading sessions as well. Many states have required lists for contests. The music supervisor may assist in acquiring contest lists for music staff, if needed.

The *Music Industry Conference Guide for Music Educators* (2001) includes a guide for ordering music products and services, which includes comprehensive lists of resources, information, and advice, such as "Your Guide for Ordering Music Products and Services" which includes "general suggestions," "print music" (including copyright laws to be aware of), "uniforms and choir robes," "musical instruments" (including specifications for all instruments), "recordings," "MIDI hardware," "computer software," "music support equipment," and "group travel."

Grant Proposal Elements

Cover Letter: If written on department letterhead and signed by the music department head or district music supervisor, letter makes a stronger case for the project.

Title page: This page names the project, project director(s), applicant organization, and date of submission or deadline for submission.

Proposal:
1. The *abstract* clearly states the project in a one-paragraph summary and includes the names/descriptions of who is involved, beneficiaries, and goals.
2. The *table of contents* lists the name of each section of the proposal with page numbers.
3. The *introduction* includes the statement of need, the objective (what is intended to be accomplished), and the significance of the project (who will be impacted by the project).
4. The *project methods* describe in detail how the project will be undertaken, including a timeline with the persons responsible, resources, and evaluation for each component.

Evaluation: Describes how the objectives will be met.

Budget: A detailed description of when and how the money will be spent.

Note. Modified from Carol A. Jones, (2001 Feb.), "Shaking the Money Tree: Fund-Raising and Grants," *Teaching Music, 8* (4), 30.

Fund-Raising and Grant-Writing

Because schools are expected to produce more "outputs" or results from student education, allocation of funds becomes more competitive. Schools increasingly take on business partners that help financially support programs, equipment, or events in a school or district. Parent/teacher organizations offer scholarships or grants to schools for innovative educational practices. Fund-raising for performing musical groups is common, and grant-writing is becoming more common. Often, supervisors will assist schools in the district in fund-raising for transportation costs, as well as for supplemental trips not mandatory to the program. In the August 2000 issue of *The Instrumentalist,* a survey of school music budgets revealed that 91 percent of school music programs participated in fund-raising. Helping teachers to find the resources they need to provide the best possible instruction for students is often a primary function of music supervisors. In "Shaking the Money Tree: Fund-Raising and Grants," Jones (2001) offers excellent advice for music educators to keep in mind in the ongoing search for funding:

- Begin fund-raising with those whom you know support you (e.g., alumni, parents, business partners, and arts patrons).
- Identify how the gifts (e.g., money, equipment) will benefit both the students and the benefactors. What will the gifts do for people?
- Carefully plan any fund-raising or grant-writing. Form the questions and find the answers to these critical questions: (1) What are the need, purpose, and expected results of the gift? (2) When do the elements of the proposal happen? (Develop a clear and concise timeline). (3) Who will be responsible for the actions? (4) What is the budget? (5) How will the effectiveness of the project be evaluated?
- Find ways to link the interests of your funding prospects to the benefits of the project. Make efforts to find out people's interests beyond their working life.
- Communication is key: write letters, make phone calls, and schedule face-to-face meetings.
- Be sure that all written communications are presented in reader-friendly format and are grammatically correct. See the Grant Proposal Elements sidebar for an outline of the critical elements and proper format for a grant proposal.

Financial Terms for Music Supervisors

Most music supervisors have had little training in financial management, other than their own personal affairs. For this reason, definitions of common financial terms that a supervisor might encounter are included in the Financial Terms Glossary sidebar.

Parting Suggestions on Finance

To keep abreast of financial concerns, supervisors are well-advised to keep these suggestions in mind:

- Pay attention to district policies for allocation of resources.
- Be mindful of what state legislators are saying and doing about education.
- Assist in educating high-level decision-makers about your activities and how the arts benefit a child's education and life.
- Establish procedures prior to start-up of school year regarding the purchasing, repair, and maintenance of instruments.
- Follow financial and business practices established by the board of education and diligently enforce them.

Financial Terms Glossary

Accounts receivable: Funds due from others for goods furnished and services rendered. Accounts payable are the funds owed to others for goods and services received and assets acquired.

Accrue: To record revenues when earned or when levies are made and to record expenditures as soon as they result in liabilities.

Accrued: Due and payable but not yet paid; accrued expenses are those that have been incurred and have not been paid as of a given date.

Advance Funding: The authority to obligate and disburse funds during a fiscal year from a succeeding year's budget or appropriation.

Allowable Charge: A generic term referring to the maximum fee that a third party payout will use in reimbursing a provider for a given service. This charge may differ from a reasonable, customary, or prevailing charge.

Allocations: A financial reporting term indicating the distribution of funds by a funding source: the assignment of revenues or costs to a cost center.

Applied Costs: The financial measure of resources consumed or applied within a given period to accomplish a specific purpose, such as performing a service, carrying out a specific project, or completing a unit of work.

Appropriation: The setting aside of funds by a legislature to pay for something authorized by law. An legislative act permitting an agency to incur obligations and make payments out of the treasury for specified purposes. Appropriations are classified by their period of availability (e.g., one year, multi-year). An appropriation ledge is used to record the account of each appropriation.

Arbitration: The means of settling a dispute by having an impartial third party (an arbitrator) hold a formal hearing and render a decision that may or may not be binding on both sides.

Audit: A review of the operations of an organization, especially its financial transactions. A desk audit is also called a job audit: a review of the duties and responsibilities of a position through an interview with supervisor and employee at the employee's desk.

Assets: The book value of items owned by the organization as reflected on the balance sheet; all the property of the person or organization that may be applied to or subject to paying off other obligations. *Current* or *liquid assets* are convertible to a known cash amount usually within a year. *Fixed assets* are those items that normally are not convertible into cash within a year (e.g., buildings, equipment, and machinery).

Budget: A plan of financial operation embodying an estimate of proposed expenditures for a given period or purpose and the proposed means of financing them, usually in three parts: (1) summary of the proposed expenditures and the means of financing them; (2) detailed schedules supporting the summary; (3) drafts of the appropriation revenue and borrowing measure necessary to put the budget into effect.

Budget, Operating: Short-term plan for managing the resources necessary to carry out a program—usually for a year, but short-term can be defined as a few weeks to a few years.

Budgetary Accounts (Proprietary accounts): Those accounts necessary to reflect budget operations and conditions, such as estimated revenues, appropriations, and encumbrances.

Capitol: Cash

Capitol Outlay: An expenditure that results in the acquisition of fixed assets or additions to

continued on next page

fixed assets presumed to have benefits for more than one year (e.g., improvements of grounds, construction of buildings, additions/remodeling of buildings, initial or additional purchases, or replacement of equipment).

Cost-Benefit Analysis: Techniques used to determine the efficiency and effectiveness of policy and program expenditures in meeting objectives.

Exempt: Not included; not obligated to pay taxes.

Equity: The mathematical excess of assets over liabilities; sometimes called the fund balance.

Fiduciary: A person who manages money or property for others (e.g., anyone who has discretionary authority or responsibility for the administration of a pension plan).

Flat Grants: A means for distributing state funds to local school districts on a per unit basis (e.g., per pupil or per teacher).

Flow-Through Budget: A financial operating plan for the handling of those funds that are distributed by a state department of education to local school districts when the state department acts only as an intermediary. Federal and state support funds are the most common examples of flow-through money and constitute neither a receipt nor an expenditure by the state department.

Full Funding: Providing budgetary resources to cover the total cost of a program or project; differs from incremental funding, where a budget is established or provided for only a portion of total estimated obligation expected to be incurred during a single fiscal year.

Fund Accounting: A traditional accounting approach used by nonprofits and many other public organizations in which separate financial records are maintained for restricted funds or groups of restricted funds and the organization's financial statements include mini-financial statements for each; fund accounting helps ensure that restricted funds are used for their intended purposes and that grant and other donor restrictions are complied with.

Fund Balance: The excess assets of a fund over its liabilities and reserves.

General Fund: Unrestricted monies and other liquid assets available for an organization's general use; a fund consisting of all receipts not earmarked for a specific purpose.

Grants: A form of gift that entails certain obligations on the part of the grantee and expectations on the part of the grantor (e.g., grants for a tax-exempt charitable foundation).

Gross Income: Total personal or organizational revenues prior to the deduction of expenses.

Liabilities: The current and long-term debts owed by an enterprise or jurisdiction. *Current liabilities* are due and payable within a year and include such items as accounts payable, wages, and short-term debt. *Long-term liabilities* are payable more than a year and include items such as bonds.

Line-Item Budget: A budgetary format wherein certain estimated receipts and expenditures appear on a given line and must be restricted to one specific purpose; such funds cannot be commingled with others.

Long-Term Debt: Debt payable more than one year after date of issue (liability).

Long-Term Debt Offset: Cash and investment assets that are specifically half for redemption of long-term debt.

Net Income: The balance remaining to a school district after deducting from the gross revenue for a given period all operating expenses and income deductions during the same period.

Operating Expense (Operating Cost): An expense incurred in conducting the ordinary activities of an organization, including running its programs, raising funds, and administering the organization.

continued on next page

Operating Ratio: Operating expenses divided by income from operations.

Operating Statement (Activity Statement): A financial statement showing an organization's revenues and expenses and budgeted and actual figures and the discrepancy or variance between them in dollars and/or percentages.

Regressive Taxes: Taxes, such as sales taxes, that decrease as the tax base increases, therefore imposing a greater burden on those persons who are less able to pay.

Tax-Exempt Status: A determination or ruling granted to an organization that frees it from obligation(s) to pay taxes and also permits donors to deduct contributions made to it.

Zero-Based Budgeting (ZBB): A budgeting process that is first and foremost a rejection of the incremental decision-making model of budgeting. It demands a rejustification of the entire budget submission (i.e., from ground zero) rather than accepting previous budgeting decisions and focusing on the margin of change from year-to-year.

Note. Modified from Jay Shafritz, R. Koeppe, & E. Soper. (1988). *The Facts on File Dictionary of Education,* New York: Facts on File.

References

2000 survey of school music budgets. (2000, August). *The Instrumentalist, 55* (1), 18–22.

Cowden, Robert, and Klotman, Robert. (1991). *Adminstration and supervision of music* (2nd ed.). New York: Macmillan.

Jones, Carol A. (2001). Shaking the money tree: Fund-raising and grants. *Teaching Music, 8* (4), 24–31.

Kirst, Michael. (1986). Sustaining the momentum of state education reform. *Phi Delta Kappan, 67* (5), 341–45.

Music Industry Conference. (2001). *Music industry conference guide for music educators: A supplement to* Teaching Music *February 2001.* Reston, VA. MENC. Copies of the guide are also available through the MENC Web site, or by calling 800-336-3768.

Rothstein, Richard. (2000). Reflections on the limitations of our ability to measure schools' productivity, and some perspective from the past. *Developments in School Finance, 1998.* Ed. William J. Fowler, Jr. Washington, DC: U.S. Department of Education National Center for Education Statistics. NCES 2000-302.

Shafritz, Jay, Koeppe, R., & Soper, E. (1988). *The facts on file dictionary of education.* New York: Facts on File.

Chapter 7
Planning

"In every enterprise consider where you would come out." This advice from Publilius Syrus (first century B.C.) Might hit a chord with music supervisors who are trying to establish a working plan for the teachers in a district. Most school districts have developed their own mission and vision statements and curriculum standards; many have established local assessments. Often, new supervisors begin their positions with many policies, procedures, and traditions in place. Establishing the need for a strategic plan for aligning the future direction of music and arts programs and anticipated activities can be a hard sell.

However, faced with ever-changing funding levels, demographics, and academic priorities, many district supervisors have chosen to create a strategic plan for their arts programs. The plan will not guarantee that the vision of the stakeholders who created it will come to complete fruition. However, the process of collecting data about what exists now in the district and discussing ways to improve and expand what exists is worth the effort. The creation of a district curriculum certainly represents a chunk of that planning. However, the development of curriculum addresses those programs that currently exist. Many other considerations and issues that help administrators and teachers determine the direction of the music programs should be considered. Some of the critical questions that supervisors might ask are the following:

1. Will the current offerings of music programs suffice for anticipated changes in demographics, such as increases or decreases in population, an influx of diverse ethnic groups, or services for special needs students?
2. Do parents and community members find the current program offerings sufficient in music and other arts? If not, what offerings should be considered?
3. Would changes in scheduling practices increase enrollment in arts classes?
4. What resources are currently used, added, or deleted?
5. How can the availability of funding be increased and stabilized to meet the future needs of students in our district?
6. How do the goals and objectives of the music department align with, support, and sustain the district's school improvement initiatives?

District music leaders play a critical role in leading planning efforts. In the early stages of developing a plan, they may be responsible for formalizing the planning process, identifying and inviting participants, scheduling meetings, establishing deadlines, and assuring that follow-up steps are completed.

Examples of Surveys and Strategic Plans

The Lincoln, Nebraska, school district collected survey data in 1993–94. Questionnaires were distributed to current and former students, parents, and elementary, middle school, and high school teachers. An example of the questionnaire given to high school teachers can be found in Appendix C. As a result of the surveys, the Lincoln district established policies and procedures that have helped stabilize and institutionalize their music programs over time.

The Los Angeles Unified School District created an arts education plan for 1999–2009. In 1997, an L.A. board of education member, in collaboration with other board of education members, convened a committee of prominent arts leaders to promote the restoration of arts education in the L.A. Unified School District. The committee urged the board of education to reinvigorate the district's performing and visual arts program. In March 1998, the L.A. board of education voted unanimously to request the superintendent to develop a comprehensive plan that would provide opportunities for all students to have a substantive education in the arts. The board also approved funds to hire a core staff of certificated arts teachers to develop a districtwide arts education program. The result of these efforts is a ten-year plan recommending goals and actions to provide a substantive education in the arts to all children.

In order to implement the plan, the district's arts education staff developed a set of actions:
- Identify and assess relevant existing policies and expectations that contribute to or impede implementing substantial arts education.
- Identify critical audiences.
- Refine vision and mission statements.
- Think strategically about a set of goals and a sequence of actions to attain those goals.
- Determine tasks that need to be done immediately and those that require later action.

The plan contained five goals, each with objectives and strategies. These were followed by an operating plan containing work tasks, timelines and budget implications for the 1999–2000 school year. For the next several years, implementation strategies would focus on developing a strong cadre of prototype schools where the arts would be taught as discrete subjects and integrated into the teaching of other core subjects. This cadre would pilot-test professional development programs and student assessments that would be refined and offered to an ever-expanding number of new schools over a 10-year period. Examples of the operational plan are found in Appendix C.

MENC's Strategic Plan

In developing a strategic plan for a school district or a music organization, music supervisors would benefit from reviewing the MENC strategic plan renewed in July 2000. The plan includes the association's mission, objectives, and strategic directions, including "Music for All," "Recruitment, Retention, and Professional Development of

Teachers," "Music Standards and Assessment," and "Partnerships and Alliances." The strategic plan can be found on the MENC Web site at www.menc.org.

Elements of a Strategic Plan

Strategic planning is a process that provides an organization or group of individuals with a framework for action. The result is a written document that guides the group toward future goals. A strategic plan includes looking ahead over the long-term, from three to ten years, and then establishing short-term strategies for accomplishing goals over the next three years.

Strategic planning is regarded as both product and process. As a process, planning is a means of promoting internal examination and facilitating future decision making. In reviewing state's music education associations' strategic plans, Lehman (2001) writes,

> The process of strategic planning is as important as the plan it produces. The very act of strategic planning is beneficial because it provides an opportunity for an association to engage its leaders and members in discussing the major issues it faces, examining its strengths and weaknesses, assessing opportunities and threats on the horizon, questioning long-held assumptions, identifying conflicts over goals or means and reaching acceptable compromises. Thus a strategic plan serves not only as a vision for the future but also as a symbol of unity of purpose within the association. (p.3)

Writing a Strategic Plan

Strategic plans most often include the following components:
- a mission statement
- an environmental scan and/or educational analysis (a collection of data regarding the current operating conditions and those predicted in the next three to five years)
- a set of goals or objectives that will direct activities for the three- to five-year period
- an action plan or set of strategies that will be undertaken in order to achieve the goals and objectives
- a set of specific actions to be taken in order to implement the strategies
- optional: a list of corresponding resources (e.g., time, money, and people)
- optional: a timeline that conveys when the actions should be completed.

Data Collection

An important first step in developing a plan is to collect data in order that future planning decisions will be knowledge-based. Knowledge-based decision-making is defined by Tecker (2001) as "an operational philosophy that ensures the consideration of information and insight in decision-making at all levels of an organization." This philosophy draws on four knowledge bases: (1) the stakeholder's views; (2) foresight about the issue area or profession; (3) understanding of the dynamics or strengths and weaknesses of the area; and (4) the ethical implications of the outcomes of the plan.

Table 1. SWOT (Strengths, Weakness, Opportunities, Threats) Analysis

	Internal Strengths	Internal Weaknesses
External Opportunities	SO: Maximize Strengths; Maximize Opportunities Strengths Opportunities	WO: Minimize Weaknesses; Maximize Opportunities Weaknesses Opportunities
External Threats	ST: Maximize Strengths; Minimize Threats Strengths Threats	WT: Minimize Weaknesses; Minimize Threats Weaknesses Threats

Several options exist for gaining understanding about the teaching and learning environment in a supervisor's community. Surveys, such as the example found in Appendix C, are an excellent data collection tool. Care must be taken in the development of surveys, however. It is a good idea to pilot-test survey questions prior to sending them out for the official survey. Confusion about the intent of a question, the meaning of a word or words, or the instructions regarding how to answer the questions is common. Also, one must ask, "What do I really want to know about my music programs, school district, or parent support?" Questions or statements should be carefully worded and focused on the intended outcomes.

Another tool for collecting data is a SWOT (Strengths, Weaknesses, Opportunities, and Threats) analysis (Crose, 1993). This tool asks respondents initially to list "(internal/external) strengths," "(internal/external) weaknesses," "(internal/external) opportunities," and "(internal/external) threats." Then, each of the categories is paired with the others, as in the chart in Table 1.

A SWOT analysis results in the formation of information cells that are cross-referenced, analyzed, and then worked into the goals and actions to be undertaken in the strategic plan. A planning committee may choose to maximize future opportunities and minimize weaknesses: a very aggressive approach. Or, the committee may determine that the best approach to future work is to minimize weaknesses and minimize threats: a less aggressive approach.

Glossary of Planning Terms

A common set of terms exists for strategic planning, whether they are used for an association, corporation, or educational institution:

action plan: a description of the specific steps and responsibilities involved in achieving an objective or goal

activity: tasks designed to accomplish strategies

goal: a non-quantified, long-range, visionary statement of intent

objective: a measurable statement of commitment to attempt to achieve a specific result

indicator: a statement of the knowledge or skills needed to meet the benchmark

stakeholders: everyone in the school community who has an interest in the education of students, is involved in, or is affected by decisions made regarding local education—including parents, students, classified personnel, certified personnel, patrons, and local business owners

strategy: a deliberate plan of action, an effective strategy, that includes a representation of an outcome, employs feedback from the environment, and takes the minimum number of steps in a particular sequence to achieve the outcome.

Collaboration Steps

Facilitating long-range or strategic planning for the music faculty may become a responsibility of the supervisor. Gordon (1997) offers a useful step-by-step strategic planning guide and examples of written plans. Included in the steps are the following:

1. Solicit support from all stakeholders for the need and scope of a strategic plan.
2. Communicate to all that the process will begin.
3. Select participants and determine the structure of the process.
4. Convene the first meeting and include the following on the agenda:
   - Select a chair (may have been selected prior to the meeting).
   - Review the purpose of the process.
   - Review the calendar of activities and timelines (e.g., when drafts and final product are due).
   - Decide when and how the plan will begin to be implemented.
   - Remind the group of local support for the planning process.
   - Establish the committee structure and operating principles.
5. Identify or create the mission statement and key decision makers.
6. Conduct data collection (environmental and teaching/learning sources).
7. Review the data and come to consensus on the goals, objectives, and strategies, based on the data.
8. Prepare, submit, publicize, and implement the plan.

Suggestions for Strategic Plan Writing

These tips can make your efforts smoother and more productive:
- Take time to have in-depth sessions to develop a mission statement, goals, and/or objectives.
- Include general categories of actions but also specific actions as well.
- Work to be consistent with the use of vocabulary. Make sure everyone defines all of the terms in the same way.
- Set a deadline for completion of activities and tasks.
- Rather than including every activity you do or will do, list focused, selective

important objectives.
- Include new staff positions under actions rather than goals.
- Do not regard the written plan as the end of the process. It is the structure for action and will be revisited regularly.
- If conditions change that warrant change, then change the plan.
- Don't assume that pre-established perspectives, procedures, or traditions should not be questioned.
- Avoid the "planning gap." Make sure there is buy-in from all levels of involvement, from students, teachers, administrators, parents, and community members.
- Put together a committee that will develop the environmental or educational scan (data collection tools).
- If possible, use an outside facilitator for your planning sessions.
- In-depth deliberations and disagreements are encouraged during the planning sessions, but once the plan is finalized, everyone should agree to support it.
- Create an implementation plan to keep work aligned with the plan. Assign a different strategy or activity to different stakeholders and ask that they be responsible for making sure specific items are addressed.
- Continue to collect data even after the plan is completed.
- Familiarize new staff and administrators with your plan.
- All meetings and activities should be tied to your plan.

References

Crose, Michael. (1993). Handout for University of Missouri–Columbia course LS410-13: "Strategic planning and budgeting" (June 21–22).

Gordon, Gerald L. (1997). *Strategic planning for association executives.* Washington, DC: American Society of Association Executives. (Web site: www.asaenet.org/am/article/1,1057,50765-feature, 00.html)

Lehman, Paul R. (2001). *Our strategic plans: How are we doing?* Paper presented at the MENC National Assembly, August 2001, Reston, VA.

Tecker, Glenn H. (2001). *Best practices in governance*: Leadership seminar for MENC National Assembly, August 2001, Reston, VA.

Chapter 8
Legal and Ethical Issues

Education is a function of government, and public school systems are a department of the government.[1] As a result, there are numerous state and federal laws that affect public and private educational institutions. Music educators must remember that each educational agency should have association with some form of legal counsel. Such counsel may occur through the administrative branch, advisory branch, or professional labor associations associated with the school district or the individual private school. Music supervisors are encouraged to be aware of their channels for legal advice and support. "Somebody told me" is not solid legal advice. Even with easy access to statutes, codes, and laws through library and Internet sources, educators are encouraged to become familiar with their personal sources of legal information and support. This chapter seeks to make music educators more aware of issues that may involve the legal rights and responsibilities of music educators and their students (for more information regarding professional ethics, consult the "MENC Code of Ethics" available on-line at www.menc.org/publications/books/ethics.html).

Levels of Legality

Music supervisors should familiarize teachers with the local sources of legal information, including policies and procedures for individual schools, the school district, and the state. In addition, federal laws may influence the structure and procedures of school programs, including music programs. Most local school policies are based on laws and procedures at higher levels, including district, state, and federal levels. However, there are times that teachers may form their own policies and procedures for individual music programs. It is important to know whom to consult and where to find information so that individual program policies and procedures do not violate the intent of more global legal decisions. This chapter addresses some of the major federal legislation from which many state and district education policies are derived. Familiarity with these laws and the issues behind the laws may assist administrators, music supervisors, and individual teachers with decisions when printed policies are not specific for a given situation.

The chapter introduces each area of legislation with references to sources of further information. Bear in mind that, while federal laws become law after a slow and arduous process, they can continue to change over time. For this reason, individual school district policies and procedures should reflect the most current state and federal laws. Advances in technology and the "information highway" have made legal information readily accessible on a variety of Web sites. Administrators, teachers, and parents now have the same access to laws and legal opinions. This creates a dichotomy with regard to policies and procedures for music education programs. When a legal question arises about a particular policy or procedure, it may be more easily resolved by referring directly to information from various legal agencies, facilitating discussion and decision making. However, the same easy access to laws governing education may cause small changes in program policies to generate debates over issues of "legality." A simple policy in which girls in a madrigal group are asked to wear matching earrings to compliment their madrigal dresses may be countered with a gender-bias opinion if the boys in the group who have earrings do not have to make adjustments. The possible issues of conflict are endless, but knowledge of laws or familiarity with sources of legal information assists administrators, music supervisors, and individual teachers as they work to develop excellence in their music programs.

Civil Rights in Education

Title VII of the Equal Rights Act of 1964 was designed for employees in the workplace. Title VII prohibits employment discrimination based on race, color, religion, sex, and national origin. The Civil Rights Act of 1991 amends the 1964 legislation to strengthen and improve the federal civil rights laws and to provide for damages in cases of intentional employment discrimination. These laws govern the workplace and have implications for music educators who are employed by public schools with regard to personal rights and responsibilities. However, this chapter focuses primarily on the rights and responsibilities of music educators with regard to their students. In the area of education, civil rights issues primarily involve the following areas: racial desegregation in schools, gender discrimination in schools, sexual harassment, equal access to education regardless of disability, due process, and school safety. In addition, music educators must be aware of legal issues involving copyright.

Historical perspective. Educators are familiar with the words "all men are created equal" from the famous document of 1776, the Declaration of Independence. The Bill of Rights (1791), with its ten major rights, was another effort to encourage equality under the laws of the United States. However, the Bill of Rights was not applied to schools at that time. In 1868, the "Equal Protection Clause" of the 14th Amendment stated "nor shall any State ... deny to any person within its jurisdiction the equal protection of the laws." But one hundred years after the Bill of Rights was written and a mere thirty years after the equal protection clause, the landmark case of *Plessy v. Ferguson* of 1892 set a precedent of "separate but equal" that would stand for more than 60 years and would have a major effect on schools.

Separate but equal. The Plessy case concerned separate train cars for black and white riders, which had been the norm. The case involved Homer Plessy, a black man who defied the laws of the land and sat in the white section of a railroad car.

Plessy was initially fined $25, but he contested the decision to the Louisiana State Supreme Court and eventually all the way to the United States Supreme Court. In 1896, the high court upheld the state's separate but equal doctrine. As a result, the *Plessy v. Ferguson* decision set the precedent that "separate" facilities for blacks and whites were constitutional as long as they were "equal." The "separate but equal" doctrine quickly extended to cover many other areas of public life, such as restaurants, theaters, restrooms, and public schools. Not until 1954, in the equally important *Brown v. the Board of Education of Topeka, Kansas* decision, would the "separate but equal" doctrine be struck down. In this case, the National Association for the Advancement of Colored People (NAACP) and the American Civil Liberties Union (ACLU) joined together to push for a change in the "separate but equal" doctrine.

What many educators may not know is that as of December 1952, the United States Supreme Court had on its docket five cases from four states (Kansas, Delaware, South Carolina, and Virginia) and the District of Columbia that challenged the constitutionality of racially segregated schools. The Court had consolidated these cases under one name, *Oliver Brown et al. v. the Board of Education of Topeka.* One of the justices later explained that the Court felt it was better to have representative cases from different parts of the country. In addition, the justices decided to put Brown first so that the whole question would not "smack of being a purely Southern one" (National Park Service, 2001). The landmark case *Brown v. the Board of Education* brought major changes in education; however, the issue of school desegregation continues to be an area of concern. School busing, urban/suburban school integration, magnet schools, and charter schools are associated with this issue. But what about "separate but equal" programs in schools? Has the spirit of *Brown* been embraced in music education?

Select Ensembles: Separate but Equal?

Today, issues of segregation may occur if students feel they have experienced discrimination due to race, culture, or gender. While "separate schools" are no longer legal, feeling separated within a school setting remains an issue for some students due to placement in self-contained special education programs, programs for speakers of English as a second language (ESOL), or "peer separation" that may result from differences in socioeconomic background, cultural background, or ability levels.

While we may not want to acknowledge it, music education programs are susceptible to such "informal" segregation. Most general music programs are "inclusive" in nature. Students from all types of backgrounds are grouped together in most elementary-level music education programs. As students enter middle school and high school, however, certain types of separation must be considered with regard to equality of opportunities. Administrators and music educators must be sensitive to the informal segregation that results when students drop out of music programs, not because of a lack of desire to participate but due to other factors. Instrumental music programs may be particularly vulnerable to such "socioeconomic segregation," including financial factors that might not allow students access to personal instruments or the private lessons that facilitate musical growth. Similar problems surface for athletic programs, even where each student is furnished with the same equipment, time for practice with specific coach/trainers, and more formalized "rules" for equality. There are no easy answers for these issues, but, as music educators, we should be challenged to consider ways to structure our music education programs so that students are not excluded by covert forms of "segregation."

Gender Issues and Sexual Harrassment

Historical perspective. Title IX of the Education Amendments of 1972 is the landmark legislation that bans sexual discrimination in schools. This law applies to all school activities, whether academic or athletic. The law states:

> No person in the United States shall on the basis of sex be excluded from participating in, be denied the benefits of, or be subjected to discrimination under an education program or activity receiving federal financial assistance. (Title IX, U.S. Department of Labor, 2001)

This law was initially applied to intercollegiate athletics. Title IX governs the overall equity of treatment and opportunity for women as a whole, not on an individual basis. Three primary areas have been the focus of Title IX in intercollegiate sports: (1) athletic financial assistance; (2) accommodation of athletic interests and abilities; (3) and assurances that all benefits, opportunities, and treatment afforded sports participants are equivalent but not necessarily identical.

Music programs are generally not troubled by the same issues with regard to Title IX as athletic programs. Generally speaking, music opportunities have been based primarily on a student's interest and ability. Under Title IX, there should be equality with regard to equipment and supplies, scheduling and practice times, travel, opportunities to receive academic tutoring or specific coaching, facilities, publicity, support services, and recruitment. The issues of gender equality within the music offerings of a school are probably not going to be an issue with regard to Title IX. However, supervisors should take note in a few areas:

1. Participation: When a school has a female group (women's ensemble) due to larger numbers of female students being interested in music, does the formation of a male group need to be offered as well? When students audition for a mixed-sex group (such as a mixed chorus) but are placed in a single-sex group (such as a women's glee club), do Title IX issues surface?

2. Clothing: Is it appropriate to require female students to purchase specific dresses and/or jewelry for a performing group if male students are allowed to wear their choice of dark suits or dark pant/white shirt combinations?

3. Travel: If the male chorus takes an annual trip but the female chorus is not also scheduled for a trip, has there been gender discrimination? If the mixed chorus or madrigal group takes a trip but the women's small ensemble does not have the same opportunity, has there been a violation of Title IX?

4. Funding: Should equal amounts be budgeted for printed music, accompanists, and so forth for gender-based groups as the amounts allocated for mixed groups? Should fund-raising activities be required of one group if it not required of all groups, especially if there are "gender" differences in the composition of the groups?

There are other examples, but the point here is that music educators must consider the implications of decisions that are made whenever there could be an appearance of gender bias or inequality. Careful consideration of equality issues should influence the planning, record-keeping, and funding of music education programs at all levels.

Harassment. Out of the issues associated with gender equity, the specific issue of harassment has surfaced as a primary concern for school administrators, teachers, and other employees. Peer sexual harassment is a complex problem that significantly affects the school environment, as well as the perpetrator and victim. Music educators must be aware of the insidious effects on their music programs of any kind of harassment. Most students do not report harassment, but surveys indicate that well over half of all students have been harassed (American Association of University Women, 1993; Shoop & Hayhow, 1994). Most frequently targeted are females, youth of color, and students identified as gay. These studies brought pressure on schools to deal with issues, especially those relating to sexual harassment.

In the 1997 *Federal Register*, the Office of Civil Rights of the U.S. Department of Education published specific guidelines in *Sexual Harassment Guidance: Harassment of Students by School Employees, Other Students, or Third Parties.* More recently, on January 19, 2001, these guidelines were published in the *Register* with revisions. Two primary areas of importance are identified with regard to the federal guidelines: "quid-pro-quo" harassment and "hostile-environment" harassment.

Quid-pro-quo harassment occurs when an offer of something is made, either asked in return for a favor or inspiring a feeling of "you do for me ... I do for you." Such harassment can occur when a school employee explicitly or implicitly grants a student a favor or, as a condition for a student's participation in an educational activity or educational decision, requests that the student submit to unwelcome sexual advances, grant sexual favors, or agree to engage in verbal, nonverbal, or physical contact of a sexual nature.

With regard to "hostile-environment" harassment, the court tends to favor the "perceiver's point of view." A "hostile" environment occurs when unwanted and unwelcomed verbal or physical contact of a sexual nature is sufficiently severe, persistent, or pervasive that it limits the student's ability to participate in or benefit from an educational activity or educational program. Music educators must be aware of any policies regarding sexual harassment that may be in place at their district or school level. If such policies do not sufficiently address issues that may occur in the music setting, then individual teachers should develop "recommended practices or policies."

Creating a Harassment-Free Environment

Music educators should avoid any situation that could be perceived as "compromising" with regard to sexual advances. Because most cases of sexual misconduct take place in private, music educators should be especially careful of situations where they provide "private lessons" or coaching. When working individually with students, an open-door policy is critical, even if it causes "noise" in the building. If possible, teachers should use a "buddy system" when assisting individual students, especially before or after school or during "planning" times when teachers are not responsible for groups of students.

Institutions can undertake three important steps to counter sexual harassment: (1) Develop strong policies that specify in writing the outlawed behaviors and penalties. (2) Establish a grievance procedure for reporting, processing, and resolving complaints. (3) Provide sexual harassment training that explains what sexual harassment means and how it can be recognized, confronted, and averted (Protecting employees, 1998).

Policies. Music educators frequently develop handbooks, policies, and procedures for their programs. Inclusion of specific sexual harassment policies banning verbal teasing, off-color jokes, improper touching, stalking, or shoving may be in order. It may be appropriate for such policies to be developed departmentally or schoolwide. When all members of an organization become involved in establishing policy, issues may be more effectively addressed and behaviors targeted. It may be appropriate for music, dance, and drama educators to work together in establishing policies because students in arts performance programs may have a different type of environment as they change costumes, apply make-up, learn dance movements, and engage in creative activities.

Grievance procedures. Developing internal procedures for reporting harassment complaints can "save time, minimize emotional and financial expense, and be more sensitive to all persons" (Brandenburg, 1997, p. 53). Effective grievance procedures should define steps for submitting both formal and informal complaints. For informal complaints, procedures should detail how the harassed person should seek advice or counsel about proper responses to offending behavior. In addition, problem-solving strategies may be outlined. The procedure for formal complaints should require that the grievance be submitted in writing and present all the facts (who, what, when, where, the scope of the incident, and names of individuals involved). Procedures should also identify the person or persons to whom the formal complaints should be submitted and explain the need for timeliness to ensure the most effective handling of the issues.

Prevention training. Educators are overwhelmed by the tasks associated with teaching. Though training in sexual harassment prevention may seem outside of the realm of music education, addressing potential harassment issues that could occur in the music setting may avert major problems at a later date. Sexual harassment can be defined as "unwanted sexual attention that would be offensive to a reasonable person and that negatively affects the work or school environment" (Brandenburg, 1997, p. 1). The key word in any definition of harassment (whether quid-pro-quo or hostile environment) is the word "unwanted." Experts agree that harassment is really about power, not sex. Students who are targets of harassment may become truant, less academically successful, and self-conscious and may develop psychological and physical symptoms (American Association of University

Women, 1993). Good music education includes providing the safe, welcoming learning environment that is so critical to maximum success for arts students.

Effective prevention programs are descriptive, intensive, relevant, and positive (Berkowitz, 1998). Though sexual harassment may be sufficiently addressed in the general school setting, music educators need to become familiar with the policies, grievance procedures, and training programs regarding sexual harassment in their own schools and in their district level. Good planning may be a critical component to a program's success. Along with issues of budget, schedules, and equipment, music educators must work to provide environments that are conducive to learning and peak artistic performance. An environment that is free of potential harassment is beneficial to any music education program.

School Safety and the Legal Rights of Students

Over several decades, issues involving Fourth Amendment rights of students in public schools have been considered by the United States Supreme Court and state courts. Such issues suggest a delicate balance between the rights of the student and the rights of school authorities to isolate and reduce perceived causes of school violence. Before 1968, the common law doctrine of "in loco parentis" (Beyer, 1997) was generally used as the basis for giving school officials the "right, duty and responsibility to act in the place of the parent," for example, to search students and their belongings for illegal items and/or items banned under local law or school policies. These searches were undertaken without the warrant or probable cause mandated for citizens under the Fourth Amendment.

From 1968 to 1984, the status shifted to a more constitutional basis. In the 1968 case of *Tinker v. Des Moines Independent School District* (1969), the First Amendment was cited as the basis for a student's right to wear a black armband in school as a protest against the Vietnam war. In delivering the opinion of the Court, Justice Fortas said: "It can hardly be argued that either students or teachers shed their constitutional rights to freedom of speech or expression at the schoolhouse gate" (*Tinker v. Des Moines*, 1969). Student "rights" became a topic for educators in many discussions on classroom management. In 1985, a major case involving the search of a female student's purse began to redefine the parameters of educators' rights with regard to search and seizure. The administrator in the *New Jersey v. T.L.O.* (1985) case had searched the purse of a female student ("T.L.O.") who was suspected of smoking a cigarette on high school property. The administrator found not only cigarettes but rolling papers, marijuana, a pipe, plastic bags, a list of students who owed her money, and two letters involving her with marijuana trading. While the court decided that students subjected to searches are covered by the Fourth Amendment, it also defined publically mandated educational and disciplinary policies as more akin to "government agents" than to "parental surrogates." A final question considered by the court was whether a warrant and probable cause are required before a search is considered reasonable. In this case, the court found that the requirement of reasonableness was met if school authorities acted without a warrant but with reasonable grounds for suspecting that the search will turn up evidence that the student has violated or is violating either the law or the rules of the school. Such a search will be permissible in its scope when the measures are reasonably related to the objectives of the search and are not excessively intrusive in light of the age and sex of the student and the nature of the infraction. (Beyer, 1997)

Thus, the court set up a two-pronged test: the search must be (1) reasonable in inception and (2) reasonable in scope.

Music educators do not seek to be "police" in the school setting. Due to the nature of working with large groups of students and frequently working with students for several years of their education, however, music educators may have closer contact with some students than other educators. Therefore, it is feasible that music educators may become aware of potential drug or weapon violations within the school setting. Appropriate consultation with administrators is desirable in any case involving student search and seizure. However, there are times when a music educator may be the primary school official in charge of a group of students. In this case, the following factors should be considered when conducting a search to ensure that it is reasonable at the inception and in scope:

1. The student's age, history, and school record.
2. The suspected infraction with regard to seriousness and pervasiveness as a school problem.
3. The level of urgency that a search be conducted without delay, noting relevant factors.
4. Prior experiences (either the teacher's or other school personnel's) with the student.
5. The eventual value and reliability of the information used to justify the search (Rapp, 1994).

A search should never be allowed if there is any question of malicious intent, discrimination, intentional violation of student rights, or disregard for school search policies. While the current climate of societal fears has brought about differences in rights for students in schools versus those of citizens outside the school setting, each student must be approached with respect and dignity.

The use of "law-related education" (LRE) is a new approach to reducing the causes of school violence through targeted educational offerings that are preventative in nature. The use of interactive instruction, with content related to rules, laws, and legal systems, helps students understand the purpose of such rules and laws. Within the music education context, the issues of providing a safe environment for artistic expression may provide an appropriate venue for teaching about the rights of the First and Fourth Amendments and of the limitations of those Amendments in school settings.

Tort Liability

Tort liability for music educators refers primarily to negligent or careless behavior that causes injury to person or property and for which the educator may be held legally liable and may be required to make compensation. Torts are civil wrongs that are distinguished from crimes in that a tort "offends some personal or property right held by the person harmed, whereas a crime is an offense against a larger social group, usually the state or federal government" (Hazard, 1979). Two broad categories of torts exist—negligent torts and deliberate torts.

Negligent Torts

A person accused of a negligent tort is being accused for failure to act or for improper action. Compensation for negligence is often based on how much the injured person should be repaid in order to make him or her "whole" again. Several factors enter into the degree to which liability is measured: (1) circumstances and conditions related to the duty of the caretaker; (2) the nature and degree of the specific care, as required by the circumstance; (3) whether the injury might have been foreseen; and (4) whether the breach of the care that was needed was the overriding cause of the injury. All four elements—duty, breach, injury, and proximate cause—must be in place in order for a teacher to be sued for tort liability. The term "duty of care," or the nature of the supervision owed by the teacher to the student, is directly related to the instructional and supervisory setting. Duty of care depends on such factors as the age, maturity, judgment, and capacities of the students and whether, based on those factors, an injury might have been foreseen under the circumstances. For instance, if a child is injured on a school stage from tripping or falling on stairs or risers, parents may issue a tort liability suit. Teachers should prepare proper lighting and remove hazards, as well as issue warnings and precautions to students. In other words, if the music teacher has exercised reasonably prudent care for the student's safety, no breach and no liability would be assigned, and the suit would likely be dismissed.

Music educators may be more susceptible to tort liability than other teachers, given the numerous opportunities for injuries in music-related activities such as field trips. Certainly, closer supervision is more likely required in out-of-school settings than in day-to-day classroom settings. The following are general principles that can assist educators in dealing with proper instruction and supervision duties:

- Always inform students of any known risks; adopt and enforce appropriate rules and regulations for student behavior; and inform parents and administrators.
- Consent forms only advise parents of planned activities; they do not reduce the duty of care owed to students or waive any liability for negligence. However, it is still a good idea to inform parents of field trips.
- Be sure that any and all means of transportation are fully insured for liability. Teachers should not transport students in their automobiles unless full liability insurance protection is carried. Never allow volunteers to drive unless they are fully insured for liability.
- Always inform students of all appropriate safety precautions for themselves, their instruments, and other equipment.
- Always provide adequate, appropriate, reasonable, and prudent adult supervision for students for off-campus school-related activities.

Deliberate Torts

Injury due to deliberate wrongdoing is much less common in schools. Deliberate torts include assault and battery, fraud and deceit, defamation of character—both written (libel) and oral (slander)— and infringement or deprivation of civil rights. In a school setting, this might include corporal punishment of a student; misrepresenting a student's academic progress to the student or parents; unjust and unfounded statements in the files that reflect adversely on a student's character, reputation, and capabilities; wrongfully suspending or expelling a student; or a teacher's or school's failure to correct known defective conditions in school equipment that lead to a student's injury.

Tort liability is different from state to state. Some states have statutes protecting teachers from simple negligence torts but allowing liability for gross negligence. Many states introduced Tort Claims Acts beginning in the mid to late '70s. Because suits for negligence are the most common school torts, supervisors should become thoroughly familiar with their state's laws.

Laws Related to Copyright

Most music educators have some awareness of laws related to copyright. MENC has been a leader in providing information regarding copyright issues to music educators; Jay Althouse's second edition of *Copyright: The Complete Guide for Music Educators* (1997) has provided an excellent sourcebook for the changing face of these laws. Other excellent sources of information on this subject that are relevant to all music education students may be found on-line in the ERIC Digest (www.ed.gov/databases/ERIC_Digests/) and in the U.S. Copyright Law, Title 17, (//uscode.house.gov/title_17.htm), which are updated frequently. However, more important than teaching students copyright laws is adherence to those laws as professional musicians and educators. Familiarity with "fair use" definitions is important, but musicians should be aware of all thirteen chapters in the United States Code on Copyrights. In the past, music educators have primarily been concerned with fair use and the ability to provide copies of articles, music, or recordings for teaching purposes. With the advent of Web-based instruction, new issues are surfacing regarding copyrights.

Current copyright law was adopted in 1976 and went into effect in 1978. The authors of the Copyright Act (1976) demonstrated foresight in their language in Section 102(a) of the law:

> Copyright protection subsists ... in original works of authorship fixed in any tangible medium of expression, now known or later developed, from which they can be perceived, reproduced, or otherwise communicated, either directly or with the aid of a machine or device. (17 U.S.C. 102)

There may, in fact, be more restrictions on the use of copyrighted material with distance education than in a classroom setting. Section 100 of the law describes the "classroom exception." This refers to a performance or display of copyrighted works in a classroom setting. The language of the law reads:

performance or display of a work by instructors or pupils in the course of face-to-face teaching activities of a non-profit educational institution, in a classroom or similar place devoted to instruction, unless, in the case of a motion picture or other audio-visual work, the performance, or the display of individual images, is given by means of a copy that was not lawfully made ... and that the person responsible for the performance knew or had reason to believe that it was not lawfully made ..., [is not an infringement]. (17 U.S.C. 1, section 110)

Such use covers most of the "teaching" aspects of music education. However, the public performance of copyrighted works may not fall into this exemption. Music educators must err on the side of caution with regard to copyright infringement.

First Amendment Rights:
Holidays, Sacred Texts, and Ceremonies

Many educators wrestle with issues associated with the interplay of religion and the public schools. Such issues may involve music educators as they choose music for public performances, choose musical activities for classroom learning, and provide music for school celebrations and activities. Over the years, increased diversity of school populations has brought issues of First Amendment Rights and religion in schools through a series of U.S. Supreme Court cases. In the 1960s, school prayer cases ruled against state-sponsored school prayer and Bible readings but upheld the practice that public school education may include teaching about religion. When seeking information about these issues, many publications demonstrate specific biases for or against their particular view of religion in schools. MENC has provided guidelines—*Music with a Sacred Text* (1996)—to assist music teachers with decisions regarding the use of sacred music in music education programs (also see www.menc.org/publication/book/relig0.html). Key to understanding the law is that the mention of religion is *not* forbidden for public school educators—what is prohibited is the advancement or inhibition of any particular religion by the state.

The best litmus test for the constitutional standards of religious neutrality comes from former Chief Justice Warren Burger in his statements from the 1971 case of *Lemon v. Kurtzman,* 403 U.S.C. 602 (1971). In order for a public school practice or policy to be considered appropriate, it must: (1) have a secular purpose; (2) have a primary effect that neither advances nor inhibits religion; and (3) avoid excessive state entanglement with religion. Students must never feel coerced by pressure from their peers or from the public to adhere to any religion nor be given the impression that their school officially prefers or sanctions a particular religion. Students may be exposed to religious music, ceremonies, or holidays as examples of cultural and historical aspects of history and the arts. However, students also must be given the right to *not* participate in any activity that violates any religious beliefs they hold. Providing alternative assignments, or allowing independent research on music education concepts/topics, may be in order.

As previously stated, student populations are becoming increasingly diverse. Schools must give special consideration to the fact that many schoolchildren belong to minority religions or are raised in a nonreligious environment. Public schools must be comfortable places for students from a variety of backgrounds, from all faiths to no faith. A spirit of tolerance, acceptance, and inclusion must prevail in music education programs in all school settings.

Special Education Laws

In the spirit of providing equal educational opportunities for all students in public schools, the issue of special education must be considered. Previous sections have discussed issues related to civil rights and discrimination based on race, color, gender, or religion, but several laws address issues specifically related to persons with disabilities and their rights to a free and appropriate public education. Most music educators have taken some type of course on the exceptional child. In their training, teachers should have learned about Public Law 94-142 (1975) and the purpose of due process, individual education plans (IEPs), and the least restrictive environment (LRE). Given the wealth of information published in music education journals regarding students with disabilities, only a brief overview of the "special-education" legislation is needed here.

Historical perspective. Music educators may not be aware of the history of special education legislation; however, civil rights activists were instrumental in the establishment of such legislation, and persons with disabilities were among those protesting in the 1960s. Following civil rights legislation in the '60s prohibiting exclusion of individuals from public services and schools based on racial differences, Section 504 of the Rehabilitation Act of 1973 was adopted (U.S. Department of Labor, 2001). This civil rights law prohibited discrimination based on disability for all programs or activities (both public or private) that receive federal funds. Essentially, this law, which is still in effect, was the first to mandate a free, appropriate public education for students who have disabilities. Moreover, it provides additional protection for students who may not qualify for special education under the Individuals with Disabilities Education Act (IDEA) (1997) but who are identified and evaluated as needing special services. For students who have difficulty in music classes—even those not placed in a special education program—there may be obtainable services to help them. This legislation also mandates that students with special needs be educated with nondisabled peers to the maximum extent appropriate.

Shortly after the Section 504 legislation was enacted, Public Law 94-142 (1975) and its update, IDEA, became law. The current IDEA is the primary legislation that governs special education in the schools. Schools are responsible for providing children aged 3–21 with special education and/or related services if they are deemed eligible (in one or more of 13 disability categories) by a multidisciplinary team. IDEA requires states to ensure the provision of "full educational opportunity" to all children with disabilities. The implication for music teachers is that "full educational opportunity" means that each child should be afforded the opportunity to participate in music education. While music teachers may teach "all" children, they may not always be provided with the "special education" support or "related services" that assist students with disabilities to take advantage of music education. Greater familiarity with these laws may give music educators the edge in obtaining assistance for such students. Music educators have every right to ask for assistance, information, and materials to support the music education needs of students with disabilities so that they can be involved in music activities at all ages. Music educators have the right, not only to know which of their students receive special education services, but to have access to those same services so that these students can have excellent experiences in music as well as other educational areas. Music educators not only have the right but the responsibility to gain access to any assistance that these students need for their education in the arts.

The Individualized Educational Program (IEP) document is an important guide to the special education process for everyone in the school. Such a guide assists teachers *and other staff* to have very specific, well-defined measurable goals and benchmarks or objectives for each eligible student. It is even more important that all teachers, including music educators, have access to the IEP when a behavior plan is included. Music educators should consider these important points: (1) If your name is on the IEP, you may be accountable. (2) The IEP manager/teacher "should" be responsible for notifying general education/mainstreaming teachers of the IEP and most definitely should notify them when there is a behavior plan for a specific student. (3) According to state law: (a) there is to be posted in the room where IEP records are stored a list of persons who can access the files, and (b) *all* student teachers are to have access to the IEP—however, the building principal determines what kind of access.

In summary, music educators are members of the teaching team for each student in their classes. As professional educators, music teachers need information and support to provide music services for each student. When a student has a disability, the music teacher needs access to the same types of information and assistance as the special education and general education teachers who work with that student. In the 1997 introduction to IDEA, Congress stated that

> over twenty years of research and experience has demonstrated that the education of children with disabilities can be made more effective by—(a) having high expectations for such children and ensuring their access in the general curriculum to the maximum extent possible, and (b) providing appropriate special education and related services and aids and supports in the regular classroom to such children, whenever appropriate. (20 U.S.C. 33, Subchapter 1, Subsection 1400, a.5.A)

Accessible music education programs and performances. The Americans with Disabilities Act (ADA) of 1990 is actually an additional civil rights law designed to prohibit discrimination with regard to employment, public services, and accommodations based solely on disability. This law has several implications for music educators beyond the typical issues of least restrictive environment (inclusion), IEPs, and due process. Music educators need to be aware of the importance of the ADA with regard to their students *and* their students' families. Student access to services is protected. The ADA gives public schools a responsibility to provide a free, appropriate public education (FAPE). This is not the direct legislation described in IDEA (Individuals with

Disabilities Act) or Section 504 of the Rehabilitation Act of 1973 (ERIC Clearinghouse, 1992). The ADA does not specify evaluation, placement, or procedural safeguards related to special education. It does, however, specify provision of reasonable accommodations for eligible students across educational activities and settings. These accommodations may include redesigning equipment, assigning aides, providing written communication in alternative format, modifying tests, redesigning services to accessible locations, altering existing facilities, or building new facilities.

Implications for music education. While music educators struggle with the issues of providing accessible "educational programming" for their students who have disabilities, the ADA addresses other issues related to discrimination and disabilities. Music educators may need assistance from administrators, district personnel, and district funds to provide the accommodations described in the ADA. Music educators should have access to interpreters for the hearing impaired if families of students in school music programs need an interpreter to experience the music program. Ramps should be provided so that students who have physical disabilities can access the stage. Audio transcription should be available for blind students or students who have visual disabilities so that they can attend ballets and concerts with their schoolmates. If students have communication boards in their regular classes or electronic adaptive communication devices for their "academic" subjects, these devices (and the paraprofessionals who assist with the use of the devices) should be available during music. There are numerous examples of the types of assistance that should be available to ensure that students who have disabilities remain integral members of the public school music education program. Music educators must be willing to make the efforts necessary to include these students.

Money Management

Music teachers are strongly advised to avoid handling monies raised by fund-raisers and other parent-teacher efforts. Often, schools begin a booster club that establishes at the outset by-laws that clearly state the organization's purpose, goals, and responsibilities (for further information, see MENC's *Music Booster Manual,* 1989). Prior to collecting any money, the booster club should establish policies and procedures for money collection operations—booster funds should always be kept separate from school funds, in a checking account that requires two signatures. A teacher should not be responsible for money in the account. Any expenditure should be approved by at least two officers of the club—preferably the entire executive committee. Booster clubs are also expected to file annual federal and state tax returns and may be subject to an audit. Therefore, they should consider establishing themselves as nonprofit and tax-exempt. Often, parent volunteers are willing to help set up a nonprofit, tax-exempt status for the booster club. In summary, it is generally recommended that the parent support group set up its own by-laws and officers, with clear delineations of which officers receive, disburse, and keep track of funds.

Conclusion

There are numerous laws that govern our decisions and actions as educators and music educators. Many of these laws are concerned with the rights of our students, the musicians whose music we use, and our own rights as human beings (laws governing our own rights as U.S. citizens and as school employees have not been discussed in this chapter). Music educators have many tasks, including becoming familiar with laws affecting education and music. Taking the time to develop policies and procedures that comply with current laws is wise; taking the initiative to develop the spirit of inclusion and fairness behind most of these laws is a different matter. Music educators can easily operate within the letter of the law and still exclude individuals from music programs by noninclusive attitudes or "artistic" exclusion. It is time to re-examine the equality of music education programs so that they provide truly excellent music education offerings and opportunities for all students. This is the true challenge of being a professional music educator.

Note

1. Much of the material in this chapter was prepared by Professor Elaine Bernstorf of Wichita State University (WSU) in Kansas, with the assistance of graduate students Sew Ping Chong, Lisa Fairbairn, Eliana Martinez, Heidi Richert, Nancy Rose, and Melissa Watkins.

References

Althouse, Jay. (1997). *Copyright: The complete guide for music educators* (2nd ed.). Reston, VA: MENC.

American Association of University Women. (1993). *Hostile hallways: The AAUW survey on sexual harassment in America's schools.* Washington, DC: Author.

Berkowitz, A. D. (1998, Oct.). How we can prevent sexual harassment and sexual assault. *Educator's guide to controlling sexual harassment, 6* (1), 1–4.

Beyer, D. (1997). School safety and the legal rights of students. *ERIC Digest,* ED 414345 1997-05-00, p. 5. (Web site: www.ed.gov/databases/ERIC_Digests/ed414345.html)

Brandenburg, J. B. (1997). *Confronting sexual harassment.* New York: Teacher's College, Columbia University.

ERIC Clearinghouse on Disabilities and Gifted Education. (1992). Legal foundations 1: Section 504 of the Rehabilitation Act and the Americans with Disabilities Act. Reston, VA: Author.

Hazard, William. (1979). *Tort liability and the music educator.* Reston, VA: MENC.

Individuals with Disabilities Education Act Amendments of 1997, 20 U.S.C. 33, subchapter 1, § 1400, Congressional statements and declarations. (Web sites: www4.law.cornell.edu/uscode/20/ch33.html and www.ed.gov/offices/OSERS/Policy/IDEA)

Lemon V. Kurtzman. (1971). 403 U.S.C. 602.

MENC. (1987; rev. 1996). *Music with a sacred text.* Reston, VA: MENC. (Web site:

www.menc.org/publicaton/books/relig0.html)

MENC. (1989). *Music booster manual.* Reston, VA: Author.

National Park Service. (2001). *Brown v. Board of Education* national historical site. (Web site: www.cr.nps.gov/nr/travel/civilrights/sitelist1.htm)

Protecting employees—and your business. (1998, Dec.). *Nation's Business, 86* (12), 18–19. As quoted in Brown, D. L. (1999). Sexual harassment interventions. *ERIC Digest,* no. 206. (Web site: www.ed.gov/databases/ERIC_Digests/ed429188.html)

Office of Civil Rights, U.S. Department of Education. (1997). *Sexual harassment guidance: Harassment of students by school employees, other students, or third parties.* 62 Fed. Reg. 12034 (March 13, 1997).

Office of Civil Rights, U.S. Department of Education. (2001). *Revised sexual harassment guidance: Harassment of students by school employees, other students, or third parties.* Fed. Reg. 5512 (January 19, 2001). (Web site: www.ed.gov/offices/OCR/shguide/)

Rapp, J. (1994). *Education law.* New York: Mathew Bender. As quoted in Beyer, D. (1997). *School Safety.*

Shoop, R. J., and Hayhow, J. W., Jr. (1994). *Sexual harassment in our schools: What parents and teachers need to know to spot it and stop it.* Boston: Allyn and Bacon.

Tinker et al. v. Des Moines Independent Community School District et al. (1969). 393 U.S. 503. As quoted in Beyer, D. (1997). *School safety.* For the complete text of Justice Fortas's comments, see the Web site: www.tourolaw.edu/patch/Tinker/.

U.S. Copyright Law. 17 U.S.C. 1 *et seq.* (Web site: www.access.gpo.gov/ uscode/title17/chapter1_.html)

U.S. Department of Labor. (2001). Section 504. *Rehabilitation act of 1973.* (Web site: www.dol.gov/dol/oasam/public/regs/statutes/sec504.htm)

U.S. Department of Labor. (n.d.). Title IX education amendments of 1972. (20 U.S.C. § 1681–88. (Web site: www.dol.gov/dol/oasam/public/regs/statutes /titleix.htm, September 3, 2001)

Chapter 9
State Supervisors

Many states have experienced drastic reductions in curriculum supervisors at the state level. Ten to twenty years ago, multiple curriculum supervisors represented the fine and performing arts areas. Generally one or more visual arts, music, and perhaps drama/theatre and dance specialists held state supervisory positions. Today, most states have a single "fine arts" consultant or one music and one visual arts specialist, if they have a person at all to oversee fine arts activities. In addition, many fine arts specialists today have responsibilities for school reform initiatives in their state. My own job position initially required 60% of my time with school reform and 40% in the fine arts. Over time, however, the emphasis has shifted to fine arts activities, as links between the fine arts and school reform initiatives in reading and mathematics have been articulated and communicated to leadership at the state and district levels.

The state supervisor's responsibilities have also changed. Most now do not see themselves as "supervisors," but as consultants or specialists. Rather than evaluating music programs in schools or recommending changes to building specifications for improved acoustics, the consultant is now more likely to spirit state initiatives such as developing state arts standards or frameworks, funding and directing state training or in-services for teachers, and leading or supporting the development of assessments or integration projects. Often, state consultants work in their state departments of education with consultants of other curriculum areas or with special education or ELL (English Language Learner) specialists to participate in agency initiatives.

Budgetary responsibilities differ from state to state as well. Many consultants receive state funding for various state initiatives or write grants in order to fund worthwhile projects. State initiatives require fairly large travel and per diem expenses for teachers or presenters who must come to the location of the event. In addition, the state consultant must carefully budget his or her travel and accommodations in order to be present at the many activities across a state. In effect, the state and local supervisors have equal challenges in terms of budget, but different challenges.

Because so many of the policies, procedures, and suggestions apply to both state and local supervisors and have been addressed in previous chapters, this chapter will highlight state initiatives currently in place across the country. Twenty state consultants voluntarily submitted descriptions of initiatives in their state that they believed would be of interest to others. They are presented here in alphabetical order by state, with contact information included.

California

The following description of California activities comes from an edited version (2001) of an electronic message from the Arts Education Partnership (aep-arts.org):

- On January 10, 2001, the State Board of Education adopted standards that for the first time spell out what students need to know to develop and demonstrate literacy in dance, music, theater, and the visual arts, just as in languages, math, science, history, and social science. Though short of a mandate, it is a step toward integrating the arts into the public schools' core curriculum.
- Admissions requirements at the state's public universities are being amended to require more arts instruction in high school.
- In February 2001, the state PTA launched "SMARTS: Bring Back the Arts," an awareness and advocacy campaign targeted at legislators, school boards, media, and parents with a goal of seeing that every public school student gets quality arts education from pre-kindergarten through grade 12. In October 2000, the 1.8 million-member organization adopted arts education as its top priority.
- Statewide, 211 school districts have received a total of $6 million in California Department of Education grants for 2001–02, seed money to help them start implementing effective arts programs.
- A ten-year arts education plan adopted by the Los Angeles Unified School District in 1999 recognizes the "powerful role" of the arts in education and has as a primary goal that every graduating senior will be proficient in one art form and have an overview of arts throughout history.

Despite signs of a revival, there are significant issues confronting the integration of the arts into curriculum. Some educators worry that the growing focus on learning that can be measured solely by standardized tests presents a threat to subjects in which assessment is more subjective. And, pressed to meet testing goals, schools may well continue to give short shrift to the arts in favor of subjects that produce hard numbers. Other issues range from a shortage of qualified teachers to ongoing financial pressures on schools.

Current developments are in stark contrast to the dark days for the arts in schools, a decline that began after passage in 1978 of Proposition 13, the property tax freeze for California. The freeze sapped funding to schools and, in the scramble for dollars, the arts were seen as frills. Schools cut programs, sold band instruments, and gave pink slips to art and music teachers. For many schools, arts education turned into a 20-year hit-or-miss proposition, a legacy not easily reversed. But arts organizations, parents' groups, and educators who have been fighting to bring back the arts feel they have won a crucial victory: a change in attitude about the importance of the arts in their own right and about the arts' ability to foster creativity and shape learning in more subtle ways.

For further information about California Arts Education Initiatives, please contact Don Doyle, Arts Consultant, California State Department of Education, 660 J. St. Suite 300, Sacramento CA 95814; e-mail: ddoyle@cde.ca.gov.

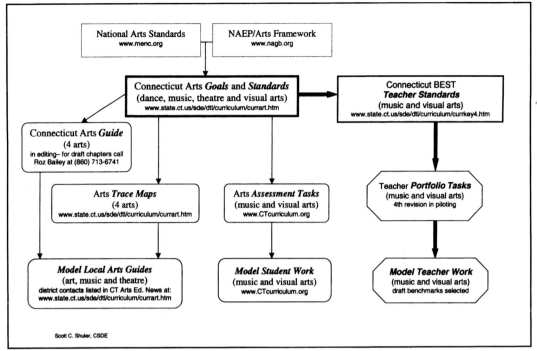

Figure 1. Connecticut Arts Curriculum and BEST Projects

Connecticut

The many projects relating to curriculum and teacher education standards are summarized in Figure 1. For additional information about these projects, contact Scott Shuler, Fine Arts Consultant, Connecticut State Department of Education, 165 Capitol Ave., Room 215, Hartford, CT 06106; phone: 860-713-6746; fax: 860-713-7018; e-mail: scott.shuler@po.state.ct.us.

Hawaii

The State of Hawaii awarded $400,000 for fiscal years 2001–02 and 2002–03 for theatre and drama, dance, music, and visual arts resource teachers for the Department of Education (12 positions at the elementary level). On July 2, 2001, Governor Ben Cayetano signed the bill into Act 306. Excerpts of Act 306 include the following:

> The purpose of this Act is to (1) continue the existence of the Hawaii arts education partners; (2) encourage the Hawaii arts education partners to persevere in its efforts to fully implement the terms of the Hawaii arts education strategic plan 2001; (3) continue the annual reports from the state foundation on culture and the arts including the reporting of the progress of the Hawaii arts education partners; and (4) appropriate funds for school-level positions in each of the four main disciplines of the fine arts, namely dance, music, theatre and drama, and the visual arts. ... The legislature recognizes and appreciates the intended goal of developing and implementing fine arts

standards is to enable every student to study and experience the fine arts by means of sequential, consistent, and meaningful arts-infused, standards-based curricula delivered by qualified arts educators, arts specialists, and artists as educators. It further recognizes and appreciates the need to augment statewide resources for and standards-based classroom instruction in all disciplines of the fine arts, particularly in the underserved areas of visual arts, music, drama and theater, and dance.

This is the fourth bill in recent years that has reached state legislative floors to provide arts instruction for all students in all the schools. This act goes beyond advocacy that focuses on general awareness and into policy dialogue, which can change the ways schools do business for student learning in arts education. An arts education partnership in Hawaii is comprised of the State Foundation on Culture and the Arts, the University of Hawaii, community arts organizations (such as the Hawaii Alliance for Arts Education), and the Hawaii State Department of Education. The state music specialist advocates for the fine arts in Hawaii and works with the legislature to get funding to support programs. One result of the partnership was a bill to fund the above fine arts resource teachers for the schools.

A "final draft" of state "performance standards" is on the Web page //doe.k12.hi.us. "Performance standards" address specific activities or indicators linked to the standards. Efforts are under way to collect student work to match performance standards and to work with teachers to assess the process, product, or performance of student work.

For more information, please contact Andres Libed, Educational Specialist for Music Education, State of Hawaii Department of Education, 189 Lunalilo Home Road, 2nd Floor, Honolulu, HI 96825; phone: 808-394-1304; e-mail: Andres_Libed@notes.k12.hi.us.

Kansas

Advocacy Initiatives: Commitments to Supporting School Reform Measures in Kansas through Music Education

Kansas music educators have worked to meet the challenges of the state's school reform initiatives through many avenues. Described in this section are a document and an ongoing statewide initative targeted at furthering the quality of arts and music education instruction in the state as well as promoting arts education as an integral part of core curriculum and the continuous improvement of Kansas schools.

tARgeTs

In 1996, a diverse group of arts educators, administrators, service center representatives, and classroom teachers gathered for the purpose of developing a document that would assist arts educators in supporting state school improvement efforts. That two-day "brainstorm" resulted in the birth of the *tARgeTS* document, which highlights the word "arts" within the word target. In Kansas, as in many states, schools are required to show academic progress in reading and mathematics—or to "target" those curriculum areas. Many educators in the state believe that the arts are essential for a comprehensive education and also play a key supportive role in better understanding other curriculum areas.

The *tARgeTS* document is now a widely used instructional strategies document that includes many examples of research-based strategies in reading, problem-solving, and assessment development. It has grown and prospered through the addition of many student work samples. The chapters include the following:

I.   *tARgeTS:* Becoming Familiar with Quality Performance Accreditation (the Kansas school reform system)
II. Responding through the Arts: Reading and Writing Strategies in an Arts Setting
III. Addressing Complex Thinking Skills and Problem-Solving through the Arts
IV. Assessing Student Learning
V.   Sources

Kansas Music PROPEL

Funded by the Kansas State Department of Education, *Kansas Music PROPEL* is an initiative that provides music educators with strategies and assessment training necessary to implement the national and Kansas music standards. Participants in the 2001 training received demonstrations of successful PROPEL projects implemented in Kansas classrooms, as well as one-on-one and small-group instruction in writing assessments for the Kansas Music Standards and the local curriculum.

The foundation for this workshop began four years ago when a group of Kansas music educators received training in Howard Gardner's Arts PROPEL instructional and assessment model and in Comprehensive Musicianship through Performance (CMP) teaching strategies. Through hard work and perseverance, these educators became trainers, not only teaching the strategies and assessments, but modeling them to music educators by using them in their own music classrooms across the state. Each year, the trainers evaluate and modify the training to fit the needs of Kansas music educators, taking the framework of Arts PROPEL (Production, Perception and Performance) and CMP (which calls for students to perform with understanding and to document the learning process) to create Kansas Music PROPEL.

Music specialists in elementary and secondary vocal and instrumental music were invited to share successful strategies for teaching the Kansas music standards. All of the PROPEL participants received valuable teaching strategies from these specialists. Each workshop participant presented a final product called a domain project at the last workshop. Domain projects are long-term, can be repeated at a higher level, include more than one type of assessment, and are linked to the Kansas music standards and QPA (Kansas school improvement model). A sample of domain projects included "Sight Reading for Choirs," "A Study of Madrigal Form and Style," "A Study of the Elements of Jazz through Performance," "Composition for General Music Students," "Integration of Music and Literature," and "Advanced Rhythm Studies in Daily Rehearsal."

For more information or to request a *tARgeTS* document, please contact Dee Hansen, Fine Arts Consultant, Kansas State Department of Education, 120 S.E. 10th Ave., Topeka, KS 66612-1182; phone: 785-296-4932; e-mail: dhansen@ksde.org.

New Hampshire

The New Hampshire Arts Framework Process

The *New Hampshire K–12 Curriculum Framework for the Arts* clearly is an initiative that has most greatly affected arts education in the state. But what is next—now that New Hampshire has adopted a framework for arts education? How does the Office of Arts Education prioritize and make decisions? How are decisions made about what work should receive coveted time and attention?

To assist all education consultants at the state Department of Education in addressing this dilemma, the department has employed the strategic planning process. In New Hampshire, the Office of Arts Education resides within the Bureau of Professional Development, one of several bureaus at the state Department of Education. The work of each bureau is guided by the organizational goals of the department. Individual work plans are aligned with organizational goals, which are revisited regularly to check for alignment and make necessary changes.

These goals are organized around seven broad areas of impact: Excellence in Teaching, Alignment of High Quality Standards-Curriculum-Instruction-Assessment, Technology, High Quality Learning Environments, Ready to Learn, Quality Data Use, and Quality of Worklife. Each area has sub-areas and related indicators against which to measure success. Whatever staff members do as an organization, as teams and as individual staff, their work must eventually align with these broader goals and measures. Additionally, our work is guided by three principles: (1) positive impact for positive improvement, based on established data and results; (2) "do-ability" for public schools, particularly through integration with other existing efforts; and (3) identification of mandated requirements of state and federal programs designed to promote educational improvement. The vision statement is "All learners meeting high standards."

To assist with this process, the organizational chart in Table 1, Criteria for Choosing Work, was developed. The rubric is used to prioritize tasks. Monthly and weekly tasks are prioritized according to a timeline as to when certain activities need to be accomplished. Granted, not every activity fits neatly within this framework, but, when needing to make a choice about activities that would appear at first blush to be time-worthy, this tool proves helpful.

One high-scoring priority from the Office of Arts Education is revising program standards in the arts to align with the *New Hampshire K–12 Curriculum Framework for the Arts*. In New Hampshire, program standards describe what beginning teachers should know and be able to do. These standards define the content and pedagogy of the teacher preparation programs. Additionally, the program standards define the alternative candidate certification requirements. In application, when teacher education programs are evaluated by visiting teams on campus, they must present evidence that their programs provide an opportunity for students to know and be able to do what is set forth in these standards.

The process of revising program standards in the arts began when the State Board of Education mandated the Professional Standards Board to revise all education standards to reflect outcome-based education. Furthermore, the revised standards were to align with state frameworks. This initiative included general education standards, professional education standards, and the program standards for each area of endorsement. The Division of Program Support at the state Department of Education provides funding.

In the arts, theatre program standards have undergone the complete process and now exist in rule-making format. Several changes were made. First, the endorsement area was changed from "speech and drama" to "theatre." Next, the program standards went from three broad statements to five outcome-based components, each with several subcomponents. Finally, these new standards align with the New Hampshire student standards in theatre. Now, the music program standards from 1984 are undergoing change.

The change model follows a method that includes involving all stakeholders in the decision-making process. Therefore, to solicit opinion from the field, the New Hampshire band directors hosted a discussion in April 2001 at the All-State music festival around this topic. The state arts consultant was asked to facilitate. The room was filled to capacity. Teachers were given the opportunity to sign up for the Music Program Standards Revision Committee. Responses from the session were

Table 1. Criteria for Choosing Work				
Factors	Level 1 Imminent (State Bd. of Ed., etc.)	Level 2 High Priority (Standards Bd.)	Level 3 Active (Inform the field)	Level 4 Pending or little time (Ind. requests from the field)
Mandate				
Potential for reaching large numbers of educators				
Potential impact on student learning				
Meets PD Bureau long-range goals				
Meets arts goals				
Good PR				
Follows national trend				
Builds partnership				

charted and used as data in the first formal meetings of the standards committee.

Opinions and committee members were also solicited from arts assessment workshops held regionally throughout the state. In this way, data were collected from all regions of the state and in a variety of settings and used to inform the decision-making of the committee.

The Music Program Standards Committee is made up of teachers from the field representing all grade levels. A member from the Professional Standards Board (who is a music educator) and a member of the Council for Teacher Education also sit on this committee. Professors from the music preparation programs in the state, along with one student, are also included. Ideally, an administrator and parent would be included. Four members were certified through one of the state's three alternative options. The state arts consultant leads the committee.

Committee time has been devoted to dialogue around issues and coming to consensus. Individuals have volunteered to create drafts on their own to share with the committee. This has been most beneficial to the process. The biggest issue facing the committee has been deciding on the context of the endorsement. In other words, should the general K–12 certification in music be retained or should the certification be split into elementary/secondary or vocal/instrumental? After several hours of deliberation and reviewing feedback from the field, the committee reached a unanimous decision to maintain a K–12 certification.

This decision was reached by consensus. The dialogue was framed around the question, "What's best for kids?" In this case, "kids" were defined as pre-K through grade eighteen. When making decisions, the committee tried to keep in mind the big picture. This includes responding to the differing needs of geographic regions within the state, determining what's best for music programs pre-K through master's level, distinguishing between music educator and musician, and understanding the impact of the critical shortage of music educators. The committee believed that education is a lifelong pursuit; professional development is vital to every teacher; every lesson about teaching cannot be garnered in the college classroom; and to be a good teacher, one must have the opportunity to teach. Therefore, a key question was: "What is the best use of one's time in a music preparation program, and what is realistic? What will best prepare beginning teachers for their profession?"

In February 2002, the committee will prepare new program standards for music education. It will present them to the Professional Standards Board. Upon approval, these standards will go to the Joint Legislative Committee on Administrative Rules. Finally, the JLCAR will present the new music program standards to the State Board of Education for their approval.

Accordingly, all music teachers seeking an initial endorsement from the State of New Hampshire will need to either (1) graduate from an approved state program of music education that abides by the new rules or (2) provide evidence of their skills and knowledge in accord with the new rules through an alternative certification option. Ultimately, all teaching and learning in New Hampshire in music education will be affected by this change. For further information, contact Marcia A. McCaffrey,

Arts Consultant, New Hampshire Office of Arts Education, 101 Pleasant Street, Concord, NH 03301; phone: 603-271-3193; e-mail: mmccaffrey@ed.state.nh.us.

Maryland

Comprehensive facilities guidelines for fine arts programs became available in 2001. These guidelines are designed to support the vision and new standards set by the community to meet the vision and new standards of fine arts education. The document includes chapters on the value of arts education, the planning process, designing fine arts spaces, and general design considerations. Copies of the facilities guidelines may be obtained by contacting James L. Tucker, Jr., Chief, MSDE Arts and Humanities Section, Maryland State Department of Education, 200 W. Baltimore Street, Baltimore, MD 21201; phone: 410-767-0352.

Massachusetts

Administrators in Music Education (AIME) is an affiliate of the Massachusetts Music Educators Association (MMEA). The mission of AIME is to provide annual in-service workshops for music and other arts administrators, teachers, and interested parties on topics relevant to arts education in the schools. The association motto is "AIME for Excellence." All music administrators in that state are automatic members of AIME without membership charge. An annual half-day fall symposium examines one "hot-button" topic or issue in depth. Areas that have been examined at various symposia include state and national arts standards, parent support groups, relationships between business and the arts, and authentic assessment.

At the annual All-State convention of MMEA in March, AIME provides many workshop sessions on administrative topics. AIME maintains a database containing contact information on arts administrators in all Massachusetts school districts. AIME is led by two state-level co-chairs appointed by MMEA. Quarterly AIME status report articles are published in the *Massachusetts Music News,* the journal of MMEA. AIME receives budgetary support from MMEA. For further information, contact Noreen Burdett, e-mail: NDiamondbu@rcn.com.

Ohio

In 1997, the Ohio Alliance for Arts Education, the Ohio Arts Council, and the Ohio Department of Education began the four-year Ohio Arts Education Assessment Project. The purpose of the project was to assist those teaching the arts as they plan and implement arts assessment of student learning in Ohio's schools. One of the project's outcomes was to provide resources that make learning in the arts more engaging, relevant, and individualized. The process guide, *The Power of Arts Assessment in Teaching and Learning,* is now available for purchase. The materials are copyrighted by the Ohio Alliance for Arts Education in the name of the partnering organizations for the projects. Please contact the Ohio Alliance for Arts Education, phone: 614-224-1060; e-mail: aaeED@aol.com (Gary DeVault, co-chair, Fine Arts Consultant

Tri-County Education Service Center, and co-chair, Project Steering Committee; and Roberta Mohan Newcomer, Music and Theatre Consultant, Ohio Department of Education, and co-chair, Project Steering Committee).

Pennsylvania

Pennsylvania does not have a statewide, large-scale assessment in the arts at present. However, several pilot programs have been set up to align arts assessment to content standards. The state is also providing consultation to local districts to set up arts assessment programs. The state's original plan, when it was going to have the statewide assessment, was to have a matrix sample of the arts standards in dance, music, theatre, and visual arts. The plan has been terminated, and the local assessment activities in the arts are required under the current Chapter 5 Regulations.

Pennsylvania has a very comprehensive *Arts Assessment Guide—Pennsylvania Assessment through Themes* (PATT), which was developed by the Pennsylvania Department of Education. It includes assessment samples from Part III of the *Guide.* Local districts can use it as a tool in the development of their own assessment tasks in the arts.

In 2001, Pennsylvania finalized a pilot project, "The Arts Assessment Sampler." Three districts—urban, suburban, and rural—each designed an assessment system for their district in the arts. These plans, the process, and the results are now available on a new Web site.

Teachers across the state have the opportunity to attend and assist in the design of the Pennsylvania Governor's Institute for Educators in the Arts and Institute for the Humanities. Each institute has a team of teachers that design, mentor, and attend. Over 500 educators in the arts have attended the institutes since 1997 and have received free graduate credit. The 1997 Arts Institute pilot led the state to design 27 others. The overall evaluations are outstanding, and local leadership has increased at the school levels in the arts.

In 2001, arts educators across the state had the opportunity to participate in the design and pilot of an on-line arts course to be offered free to Pennsylvania teachers. All of the department projects seek participation from music and arts educators, administrators, and higher education professionals. The Pennsylvania Department of Education advisor sends the "PDE Arts Update" to the field in hard copy and via e-mail three times a year and announces various opportunities for participation in department projects and national or other funding sources. For more information, please contact Beth Cornell, Fine Arts and Humanities Advisor, Pennsylvania Department of Education, 333 Market Street, 8th Floor, Harrisburg, PA 17126-0333; phone: 717-787-5317; fax: 717-787-7066; e-mail: bcornell@state.pa.us.

Rhode Island

"Literacy in the Arts—A Framework for Action" is a culmination of eighteen months of public meetings, research, and deliberations of the governor's Literacy in the Arts task force, created to "examine the relationship between education reform and the arts, and to make policy recommendations on how the arts can have a significant impact on the educational agenda of Rhode Island." For more information about the framework, please contact Peter McWalters, Commissioner, Rhode Island Department of Education, P.O. Box 1613, Providence RI 02901-1613.

Texas

The second annual Texas Fine Arts Summit was held on June 14–15, 2001, in San Antonio. Sponsored by the Center for Educator Development in Fine Arts (CEDFA), the summit is a collaborative project of the Texas Education Agency (TEA), Education Service Center, Region 20 (ESC-20), in San Antonio, and the Texas Commission on the Arts. CEDFA, housed at ESC-20 and funded by TEA, is a project to promote student achievement in the fine arts by defining and supporting quality professional development for Texas educators, based on the fine arts Texas Essential Knowledge and Skills (TEKS), the state learning standards for fine arts aligned with the National Standards for Arts Education. CEDFA has identified the following four goals to direct the center's actions: (1) facilitate systemic change through the implementation of the fine arts TEKS; (2) provide a coordinated, statewide fine arts network that supports leadership in the implementation of the fine arts TEKS; (3) strengthen fine arts instruction through quality professional development based on the TEKS; and (4) increase student achievement in art, dance, music, and theatre.

The primary focus of the 2001 Summit was performance assessment as related to the fine arts TEKS. Other fine arts instructional areas included interdisciplinary instruction and technology integration. Presenters who are members of the CEDFA training cadre conducted workshops and demonstrated best practices in each of these three topics for art, dance, music (band, orchestra, choir, and elementary), and theatre. The training cadre is comprised of identified master teachers who participate in annual "trainer of trainers" sessions sponsored by CEDFA in preparation for the state fine arts summit. Names of cadre members are provided to regional ESCs and school districts statewide as highly qualified fine arts education experts who have been trained by CEDFA in workshop presentations. Other summit highlights were as follows:

- A new feature of the CEDFA Web site (//finearts.esc20.net/), which contains valuable information and resources for fine arts educators, was announced: "Connect the TEKS," a tool that allows users to link with relevant on-line Web sites that can be utilized according to subject area and grade level in conjunction with each of the four strands of the fine arts TEKS (perception, creative expression/performance, historical/cultural heritage, and response/evaluation).
- A second fine arts video series, "Proof of Performance: Fine Arts in Texas Schools," produced by TEA in conjunction with the T-STAR Communications Network, Buckalew Media, and CEDFA, was previewed, and each participant received a complimentary copy in a fine arts subject area of choice. The videos feature exemplary fine arts teachers and programs with particular emphasis on assessment strategies in the arts as related to the fine arts TEKS. The series of

four videos covers each of the fine arts disciplines (art, dance, music, and theatre) while representing all grade levels, geographic regions, socioeconomic backgrounds, ethnicities, and school-district sizes throughout the state of Texas. As is the case with the first video series titled "Fine Arts Education: Portrait for Excellence" produced during the 2000–01 school year, the new videos are available for check-out from all regional ESCs or purchase from CEDFA as a valuable instructional resource and professional development model for teachers and administrators to enhance fine arts education in the public schools.

- A working draft of a document titled "PDAS and Fine Arts Teachers" was provided to participants for feedback. This set of guidelines was developed by TEA and CEDFA to assist school administrators when appraising fine arts teachers in Domain VIII of the Professional Development and Appraisal System (PDAS), which relates to skills students must demonstrate on the Texas Assessment of Academic Skills (TAAS). Upon completion of incorporating the suggestions of summit participants, the "PDAS and Fine Arts Teachers" document will be mailed to all Texas school districts and will also be available to download from the CEDFA Web site.

For additional information regarding the Texas Fine Arts Summit, please contact Thomas H. Waggoner, Director of Fine Arts, Texas Education Agency, 1701 N. Congress Ave., Austin, TX 78701-1494; phone: 512-463-4341; fax: 512-463-8057; e-mail: twaggone@tea.state.tx.us.

Utah

Every other year, the state of Utah sponsors a two-week retreat for teams of classroom and arts teachers and administrators. This retreat, called "Pieces of One," immerses the teams in visual art, music, drama, and dance experiences as a means of teaching them to prepare their arts-in-education instruction for students in the following school year. Retreat goals are to provide resources, experiences, understanding, and tools that enable participants to be successful in their specific roles as educators and to support the development of new friendships, networking, and support for continued personal and professional growth. The catalyst for creativity and study throughout the retreat is nature.

The learning targets for the retreat fall into five categories: (1) an intelligent overall understanding of dance, drama, music, and visual arts as expressive arts, disciplines, motivators, and tools for other learning; (2) an understanding of how the arts reveal us to ourselves and cultivate genuine mutual respect, self-worth, and a valuing of personal identity and connections with each other; (3) a grasp of some of the fundamental elements and skills that are part of dance, drama, music, and the visual arts; (4) a vision of how to effectively teach *in* the arts, by focusing on them *as* curriculum, as well as teaching *through* them and *about* them; (5) a practical long-range plan for implementing the arts core curriculum for each school as a means for providing a healthy balance in each child's educational experience by providing specific plans for the coming year. Examples of units of study include "Cycles—Music in Nature, Nature in Music" (music); "Introduction to the Master Work" (visual arts); "Cycles—Nature's Dance" (dance); and "Animals within Us" (theatre). For more information about "Pieces of One," please contact Carol Ann Goodson, State Fine Arts Specialist, Utah State Office of Education, 250 East 500 South, Salt Lake City, UT 84111; phone: 801-537-7793; e-mail: cgoodson@usoe.k12.ut.us.

Vermont

Vermont Arts Assessment Project—Focusing on the Nature of Artistic Practice in Learning, 1993–96

The work of the teachers in the Vermont Arts Assessment Project was in progress for almost three years. Teachers came to the project for a variety of reasons: to raise the standards for arts education, to pursue an interest in advocacy for arts in general and the relationship between advocacy and assessment, to tie into the general portfolio initiative of the state of Vermont, or to improve the quality of their own instruction. The project was made possible by the generous support of the Jessie B. Cox Charitable Trust, the National Endowment for the Arts, and the Vermont Arts Council. One result of the project is a booklet that addresses areas such as skill development, reflection and critique, making connections within and across disciplines, approach to work and classroom, and assessment tips; this booklet may be obtained by contacting Vermont Arts Council, 136 State St., Drawer 33, Montpelier, VT 05633-6001. The booklet is also available on-line at www.vermontartscouncil.org/resources/publications.html.

Vermont Music Performance Benchmarking Project, 1998–99

Participants in the Vermont Music Performance Benchmarking Project worked for one year. These music educators came to the project for many reasons but shared one goal—to fill a major gap in the state's almost-complete, standards-based music education package by creating "user-friendly" benchmarks for the evaluation of musical performance. The resulting booklet and cassette tape can be used to enhance the work of the Vermont Arts Assessment Project. The booklet includes the process of the project, the examples and descriptions of the benchmarks, practical uses, a glossary of terms, and a detailed scoring guide. Funding for this project was obtained through a Goals 2000 grant through the State of Vermont, through the U.S. Dept. of Education. Both the booklet and cassette may be obtained by contacting Tony Pietricola, 6 Old Town Lane, Grand Isle, VT 05458; phone: 802-372-5363, e-mail: tonyvje@aol.com.

Vermont MIDI Project, 1995–present

This project's Web site allows student musical composers to post their work on-line so that other participating schools, teachers, students, and professional composer/mentors can have access and offer constructive criticism for the purposes of critique and revision. Presently, approximately 46 schools are actively participating. For more information, please go to the project's Web site (www.vtmidi.org) or contact the project administrator, Sandi MacLeod, at sandimac@adelphia.net.

Virginia

Virginia Music Standards of Learning Background and Process

Members of the Virginia Board of Education voted unanimously on February 25, 1999, to request a work plan for the revision of the 1983 Music Standards of Learning. A revision of the Music Standards of Learning had been done in 1987, but that revision was never taken to the Board for approval. The work plan for revising the Music Standards of Learning was approved during the Board's annual retreat on April 29, 1999.

In November 1999, a draft of the revised Music Standards of Learning was distributed to the 1,000 participants in the Virginia Music Educators Association's Annual In-Service Conference. A feedback form and a summary of the Music Standards of Learning revision process were attached to the draft. Comments received on the feedback form were used to finalize a draft document for the Board of Education dated December 20, 1999. This draft was presented to the Board of Education for first review on January 6, 2000. The Board accepted the draft, and five public hearings were scheduled for April 3, 2000. Public comment from these hearings was documented for the Board. A subsequent draft was presented to the Board of Education for final review and approval on May 26, 2000. The revised Music Standards of Learning are posted on the Web (www.pen.k12.va.us/VDOE/Instruction/Music/musicl.html).

Standards of Learning for art, dance, and theatre were revised simultaneously and placed with the Music Standards of Learning in a unified document, the Fine Arts Standards of Learning. Each division-level superintendent received a hard copy. Additional hard copies were sent to the principal, media specialist, and arts teachers in each school. This document was also disseminated at the respective state arts conferences during the fall of 2000. The Fine Arts Standards of Learning document is posted on the Web (www.pen.k12.va.us/VDOE/Instruction/sol.html).

Writing Committee Selection

A memorandum from the State Superintendent of Public Instruction was sent to each division-level superintendent. This memo included a copy of the workplan for the Music Standards of Learning revision and a nomination form to allow superintendents to submit names of individuals to serve on the Music Standards of Learning Revision Writing Committee. The names of the individuals selected to serve on the Steering Committee were announced at the Virginia Music Educators Association (VMEA) Executive Board meeting, June 5, 1999.

Profile

The 24 individuals who were selected to be on the Writing Committee represented all 8 of the Superintendent's Regional Study Groups. The Music Standards of Learning Writing Committee was comprised of 8 Steering Committee members and 16 additional members. For the revision process, the Writing Committee was divided into 3 groups: Music K–12; Instrumental; and Vocal/Choral. One division-level specialist and one representative from higher education were in each of the three groups. One principal, a former music supervisor and music teacher, was a member of the Steering Committee. One classroom teacher and one individual from higher education were in each of the 3 groups of the Steering Committee. Three of the 8 Steering Committee members were classroom teachers, and 14 of the 16 additional Writing Committee members were classroom teachers. Seventeen of the 24 Writing Committee members were classroom teachers. Eight members of the Music Standards of Learning Writing Committee were serving or had served as officers in VMEA. Three Steering Committee members served on one of the three VMEA Learning Standards committees: one on the General Committee; one on the Review Subcommittee; and one on the Steering Committee.

Procedure

The Steering Committee first met at Shenandoah University on June 22, 1999, and made some preliminary decisions that were subsequently endorsed by the Writing Committee on July 18, 1999:

- Music Standards of Learning would be written for each grade level K–5 and for two non-performance clusters, 6–8 and 9–12.
- Instrumental Music and Vocal/Choral Music Standards of Learning would be written for four levels—beginning, intermediate, advanced, and artist.
- All Music Standards of Learning would be written as benchmarks and organized by four strands—Perform, Create, Investigate, and Connect.

The full Writing Committee met July 18–23, 1999, at Shenandoah University to revise the Music Standards of Learning. Four parents and four students worked with members of the Writing Committee. The Steering Committee provided leadership to the Writing Committee. For the revision process, the Writing Committee used the 1983 and 1987 Virginia Standards of Learning for Music, the National Standards for Music Education, the VMEA Learning Standards, and standards or comparable standards documents from other states. The Writing Committee documented all revisions made in reference to the 1983 Music Standards of Learning and the 1987 revision in a crosswalk format. Writing Committee members correlated the revised Music Standards of Learning with Virginia Standards of Learning in English, Mathematics, Science, and History and Social Science. In addition, correlations were made between the revised Music Standards of Learning and the National Standards and VMEA Learning Standards. The Music Standards of Learning, as well as the crosswalks and correlations, are posted on the Web (www.pen.k12.va.us/VDOE/Instruction/Music/musicl.html).

For further information, contact Theresa Lee, Music Specialist K–12, Virginia Department of Education, phone: 804-786-8078; e-mail tlee@pen.k12.va.us.

Washington

The arts are part of Washington State learning goals:

- Arts Essential Academic Learning Requirements (standards) and Arts Frameworks (what all students should know and be able to do in the arts) have been developed.
- Statutory timelines for state arts assessment have been developed: middle and high school—voluntary 2005–06 and required 2008–09; elementary school—voluntary 2005–06 and required 2009–10.
- New teacher certification standards in dance, theatre, music, and visual arts have been codified.
- An ongoing biennial conference, *Arts Time All the Time,* co-sponsored by Dance Educators Association of Washington, VSA Arts of Washington, Washington Alliance for Arts Education, Washington Alliance for Theatre Education, and Washington Music Educators Association, is facilitated by the State Supervisor of Visual and Performing Arts.
- A 2001 professional development summer institute, "Creating Connections: The Arts, Learning and Successful School Institute" (CCLASSI), was sponsored by Washington Alliance for Arts Education and facilitated by the State Supervisor of Visual and Performing Arts.

Wisconsin

Implementing the Standards with the Arts PROPEL

Three developments in music education in Wisconsin and across the nation are broadening the scope of performance groups. Prior to the mid-'70s, almost all school music programs were based solely on performance, and the mode of teaching was direct teacher instruction. Understandings were gained through such programs but were usually quite narrowly focused on performance technique. In 1977, Mike George, then state music consultant at the Wisconsin Department of Public Instruction (DPI); Richard Gaarder, executive director of the Wisconsin School Music Association (WSMA); and a committee of Wisconsin music educators developed an instructional model, Comprehensive Musicianship through Performance (CMP), which was designed expressly to broaden musical understandings beyond performance skills using the rehearsal as a learning lab and the music being performed as an instructional vehicle.

Comprehensive Musicianship through Performance

CMP is based on five principal areas of concern in performance instruction: outcomes, music selection, analysis, strategies (instruction), and assessment. While teachers can begin with any of the five points, one possible progression would be to establish desired outcomes; select a composition to reflect those outcomes; analyze its central focus, style, and historical and technical points; and then plan teaching strategies and assessment procedures. As an example, a conductor who wishes to emphasize learning about the Baroque, certain compositional techniques, or a composer (outcomes) would choose music illustrating those points (music selection), carefully study its various illustrative qualities (analysis), plan instruction to achieve understanding of them (strategies), and prepare ways to determine student mastery (assessment). This practical approach allows the music being prepared for concert performance to be the instructional vehicle.

Student involvement throughout the process is important and extends to the concert performance itself. Students research and write program notes; arrange motivic demonstrations for the audience to clarify a composition's form and structure; describe important historical or stylistic features; or detail the various activities and learning experiences in which the group was involved. Such performances are often called "Informances." More complete information on CMP may be obtained from the WMEA office: Jan Tweed, phone: 608-249-4566, or Mel Pontious, phone: 608/267-5042.

Arts PROPEL

A second development was the work in the late '80s of Harvard Project Zero, Educational Testing Service, and the arts faculty of Pittsburgh schools in developing Arts PROPEL, an instructional/assessment model that focuses mainly on producing (performing, creating), perceiving, and reflecting (responding). The model emphasizes active student involvement in all stages of learning and assessment.

Certain elements distinguish the PROPEL model of instruction/assessment: applying constructivist teaching/learning practices; fostering intrinsic motivation through teaching strategies; using open-ended problems (no single right answers); employing a mix of closely structured and relatively unstructured learning activities; and involving students in a "learning loop"—producing, perceiving, and reflecting.

Two teaching vehicles were developed during the research—domain projects and processfolios. Since the construction of deep understandings does not easily fit into a given time period, long-term learning units—domain projects—were found to be necessary. These are open-ended tasks (performing, composing, etc.) that require the application over time of previously acquired knowledge and skills. They can (should) be authentic, real-life tasks that have no single, correct answer, challenge and motivate students to pursue solutions, engage students in production and perceptual and reflective experiences, require students to function as practitioners in the domain instead of pursuing a set solution, and, ideally, allow students to help design.

For instance, a teacher who wanted to enhance the students' performance levels could regularly engage students in analyzing taped sections of rehearsals and suggesting improvements. Prior to the project, the teacher and students would decide on the important points to consider, in both performance and critiquing, and on what would constitute "good," "outstanding," and "not quite" proficiency levels in both areas. Through this, students internalize the learning targets and gain a sense of ownership. Supportive teacher comments on both performance and critiques reinforce student judgments that were on target and serve as a guide for those wide of the mark. This "learning loop"—producing (performing), perceiving (analyzing the performance), and reflecting (evaluating, suggesting improvements)—is consonant with research on optimal learning.

In order for students to analyze and reflect on their work and process over time, processfolios (process portfolios) were instituted. These contain the students' work from the beginning to the end of the domain project and form an excellent basis for the students and teacher to see progress in both product and process. Such self-assessment was shown to be more effective in enhancing deep understanding than direct instruction. More complete information on Arts PROPEL can be obtained from Harvard Project Zero literature by contacting Mel Pontious, phone: 608-267-5042; e-mail: melvin.pontious@dpi.state.wi.us, or on-line at www.pz.harvard.edu/Default.htm.

Music Standards

Finally, the standards initiative, both at the national level and in Wisconsin, has emphasized, deepened, and affirmed the movement to make music education more comprehensive. Besides the more factual understandings in the areas of history, culture, the musical forms and strategies used by the composer, the relationships with other disciplines, and so forth (Standards 8 & 9, "knowing about"), the National Standards for Music Education also focus directly on the processes of performing, creating, and so forth (Standards 1–7, "knowing how-to-do").

CMP, Arts PROPEL, and the Standards

The relationship of CMP and Arts PROPEL to the music standards can best be explained in terms of the two kinds of "knowing"—knowing about music (declarative knowledge) and knowing "how-to-do" music (procedural knowledge). Each model has unique aspects that are complementary when used to implement the music standards:

- CMP was developed to expand the traditional focus on performance skills to include understandings about music as well as performance. Teachers using it still taught performance skills, of course, but CMP especially enriched students' understandings about the music being performed.
- Arts PROPEL's instructional/assessment strategies are based on how humans learn most naturally and focus especially on helping students develop independence and expertise in learning how-to-do music (procedural knowledge) in all "musicianly" areas, including performance.
- The Music Standards reinforce CMP's emphasis on declarative knowledge (especially Standards 8 and 9) but, like PROPEL, also address procedural understandings beyond performance, to include improvising, composing, notating, analyzing, and evaluating (Standards 1–7).

A logical use of the two models in implementing the standards is to employ the CMP framework and utilize the PROPEL strategies and vehicles of instruction/assessment (production, perception, reflection; domain projects; and processfolios) when developing the "strategies" and "assessment" sections of CMP.

Implementing the Standards

This is a possible scenario: using the CMP approach, the teacher selects quality music for performance that can also serve as a study text to address selected content and performance standards (Outcomes). For instance, students can gain understandings about the music (Standards 8 and 9) by researching aspects of the music such as form, style, compositional techniques, historical milieu, relationship to other arts and disciplines, and so on, in order to prepare program notes and/or demonstrate the compositions' structures to the concert audience. Knowledge such as this can enrich each listening and heighten students' aesthetic responses. At the same time, students can use the PROPEL strategies to address the "how-to-do" Standards (1–7), such as aurally analyzing and evaluating tapes of their rehearsal performances (Standards 6 and 7) with supportive peer and/or teacher feedback. Or, if the music was selected as an example of improvisational or compositional techniques, students could improvise or compose (Standards 3 and 4), using the music being rehearsed as a model. [The student self- and peer-assessment part of the PROPEL model (perceiving and reflecting) coincides exactly with Standards 6 and 7, aurally analyzing and evaluating.]

Assessing Student Progress

Assessment would occur as a matter of instructional practice. By involving the students regularly in self- and peer-assessment and by responding to their assessments and products, the teacher embeds assessment in an ongoing way in instruction. The students' assessments and the teacher's response to them give students a continuing view of their progress so they can direct their efforts more efficiently. This also helps the teacher facilitate the students' efforts more effectively. And, as noted above, by specifically asking (and respecting) the students' opinions, the model fosters intrinsic motivation and active student involvement in learning.

An important point is that one can't claim to have taught the standards effectively unless two things occur: (1) The students know the targets of learning beforehand ("What are we expected to learn in this project and at what level of proficiency?" The students should be part of the discussion that determines this). (2) The students know if they are "getting there" (or, at the end, if they got there) and why—mere exposure is not enough. And they should learn this through ongoing assessments (as above)—self, peer, and teacher—embedded in instruction.

Wisconsin Arts Assessment Project

This project combines the Comprehensive Musicianship through Performance (CMP) and the Arts PROPEL models of instruction/assessment. It is a two-year action research project focused on the question "How can music educators implement the standards in a substantive way that motivates students to become actively involved in their learning?"

Rationale. True assessment must be done in the context of a student's actual performance of a task, and this is only feasible in the local setting by the one who knows the student's abilities and capabilities best—the teacher. This is the basis of this action research project, which focuses on helping teachers develop examples of student work at the different proficiency levels, much as the adjudicator workshops do for festival judges. Teachers report that it has a multiple effect—helping teachers establish a common concept of the different proficiency levels of the various standards and developing protocols for direct assessment that (1) embed assessment in instruction; (2) engage students actively in their own education; and (3) establish assessment as a comfortable, even sought after, aspect of learning.

Procedure. A group of 40 arts educators—20 each of music and art—met during an all-day workshop in February 2001 and planned (1) common instructional projects based on selected standards; (2) instructional strategies; and (3) assessment protocols embedded within the instruction. They implemented them with their students during that semester and met again in June to discuss their successes and challenges; examine representative student work and establish proficiency-level benchmarks; and develop other instructional/assessment projects, based on selected standards, to implement during the 2001 fall semester. They meet three to four times each year to discuss teaching strategies, student work, and benchmarks and to plan further projects. They devised the projects to coincide with the normal work of the classroom or rehearsal. If the standards selected for a performing group were 3, 6, and 7, the students and teacher would decide on the important focal points of each area (improvisation and analysis/evaluation) and the proficiency levels (rubrics) for each area. The teachers assess the students' critique of their performances and give supportive guidance on performing and critiquing. Assessment is based on teacher/student-developed rubrics dealing with the previously determined criteria for improvisation and analysis (e.g., authentic style; accurate harmonic changes; accurate and detailed error detection; specific references to locations in the score; use of music terminology; suggestions for revision; and linkage of suggested solutions to the indicated problems).

Besides enhancing classroom instruction, such assessments across the state could provide a true statewide picture of the status of music education while avoiding the distortion and shortcomings of large-scale high-stakes testing. Other outcomes might be benchmarks of student work in relation to the standards, examples of long-term projects based on the standards, effective assessment protocols, and a cadre of teachers who can train others. For further information, contact Mel Pontious, State Music Consultant, WI Dept of Public Instruction, P.O. Box 7841, Madison, WI 53707-7841; phone: 608-267-5042; e-mail: melvin.pontious@dpi.state.wi.us.

Appendix A: Supervisor's Job Descriptions

Lincoln Public Schools
Supervisor of Music
Responsibilities

*Curricular Responsibilities: **(These are typical Curriculum Specialists responsibilities.)**
  -**Direct** Curriculum Review (5-9 year process)
  -**Advise** principals on curricular and staffing matters
  -**Advocate** for music
  -**Represent** LPS and the music department in the community and state
  -**Plan**/conduct Staff Development and inservice
  -**Liaison** between LPS and UN-L, UN-O, NWU, and community arts
     organizations
  -**Support**, promote, and implement district initiatives, e.g. interdisciplinary
     instruction, middle level education, multicultural education,
     inclusion, etc.

xxxxxxxxxxxxxxxxxxxxxxxxxxxxxxxxxxxxxxxxxxxxxxxxxxxxxxxxxxxxxxxxxxxxxxxxxxxxxxxxxxxxxxx

Supervisory Responsibilities
**(These responsibilities represent duties that are akin to some
building principal responsibilities, as well as some
activity director responsibilities. Please note that
LPS Curriculum Specialists do not typically perform any of the following duties.)**

*Hire, Assign, Supervise and Appraise 28 certificated staff members (the instrumental
itinerants and string specialists)

*Hire, Assign, Supervise and Appraise 18 piano accompanists

*Oversee the repair of LPS-owned instruments

*Maintain an inventory record of all LPS-owned instruments

*Supervise and Appraise one office secretary and one music librarian and oversee the
operation of the music library

*Organize and produce 14 all-city music festivals/contests/concerts each year
     -This includes the following responsibilities:
          1. Securing sites
          2. Hiring judges/clinicians
          3. Printing programs and tickets where needed
          4. Transferring equipment
          5. Paying for rented facilities
          5. Paying judges/clinicians
          6. Hosting these events

1. **Invitational** Marching Band Contest at Seacrest
   19 Bands, 5 Judges, and other workers
2. **High School** Orchestra Night
   4 Orchestras
3. **Vocal** Solo Recital
   20 Singers and 2 Clinicians
4. **Middle School** Instrumental Music Festival at Pershing
   2 Guest Conductors
5. **High School** Choir Festival at the Lied
   5 Choirs and 3 Judges
6. **High School** Instrumental Solo/Ensemble Contest
   5 Judges
7. **High School** Jazz Festival
   10 Bands and 5 Judges/Clinicians
8. **Middle School** Solo/Ensemble Contest
   15 Clinicians
9. **Middle School** Choral Festival
   1 Guest Conductor
10. **High School** Band Contest
    4 Bands and 3 Judges
11. **Elementary** All-City Festivals (3 nights)
12. **High School** Madrigal/Small Ensemble Night
13. **Middle School** Orchestra/Jazz Band Contest
    2 Judges
14. **Middle School** Band Contest
    1 Judge

*Approve and arrange bus transportation for high school music ensembles

*Supervise the following All-City Ensembles
-Lincoln Youth Symphony
   1 director and 3 coaches
-Junior Youth Orchestra
   1 director and 2 coaches
-SOKS Orchestra
   2 co-directors
-All-City Girls Choir
   1 director, 1 assistant director, and 1 accompanist

*Manage Music Department Budget of $183,000 (Parts of which are allocated to all 106 music teachers in 50 buildings.)
-**Monitor** teachers' spending
-**Prepare** equipment and supply cycle requisitions
-**Revise** equipment and supply catalogs
-**Purchase** $60,000 worth of sheet music annually
-**Purchase** $90,000 worth of instruments and equipment annually

Music Education State Consultant

Position Summary:

The main role of this position is to provide statewide supervision and leadership in music education . This is accomplished by: 1) promoting DPI programs and policies; 2) consultation, inservice presentations, and position papers; and 3) by working with professional education organizations, state and local agencies, colleges and universities, districts, and teachers. This necessitates staying current with relevant national research and educational practices and generating initiatives that will enhance music education in Wisconsin. An integral aspect of the above point is maintaining contact with thte field by acting as a liaison to various constituencies and responding to requests for information from educators and community members.

Goals and Worker Activities:

40%
A. Supervision and Leadership
1. provide leadership in the development and implementation of curriculum, instruction and assessment practices, and state level standards in music education.
2. Initiate inservice opportunities for teachers related to curriculum, instruction, and assessment in music education.
3. Initiate teacher-led inquiry, experimentation, and innovation in music education.
4. Communicate with school administrators, school boards, and community groups relative to music education and comprehensive arts education.
5. Gather data on school music programs and disseminate information to appropriate school personnel.
6. Inform college and university staff of school music programs and practices which have implication for their curricula.

40%
B. DPI Programs and Policies
1. Provide supervision and consultation regarding the educational standards.
2. Promote such programs as Connecting the Curriculum Challenging Content Standards, CMP, Arts PROPEL, ASBEG, and others as they relate to music education.
3. Participate in DPI reviews of teacher training programs.
4. Recommend needed changes in PI-4.
5. Cooperate with the University's Department of Continuing Education in the Arts and the University System in initiating programs.

State Music Consultant Continued:

20%
C. Liaison Activities
   1. Serve on the Boards of the Wisconsin Music Educators Association and the Wisconsin School Music Association and support their various activities.
   2. Provide leadership to arts related groups such as the Wisconsin Alliance for Arts Education, the Wisconsin Arts Board, the Wisconsin Society of Teacher Educators in Music, the Association of Wisconsin College and University Music Administrators, the Wisconsin Association of Music Supervisors, and others.
   3. Represent the Wisconsin Department of Public Instruction on national music and arts education associations.

Appendix B: Contest Forms

LPS MARCHING BAND CONTEST CHECK LIST

October 13, 2001

___Send expense sheets to judges. (take extra blank ones)

___Send contest order, program information sheets, and final instructions to bands.

___Order trophies.

___Print programs

___Hire policemen.

___Hire ticket sellers and takers.

___Hire first aid.

___Get ticket rolls.

___Get change.

___Print rating sheets.

___Send complimentary tickets to band directors.

___Make sure U.S. Flag will be flying.

___Make Name Tags

___Order Tapes

Dear Band Director:

On Saturday, October 13, 2001, the 21st annual Lincoln Public Schools Invitational Marching Band Contest will be held at Seacrest Field in Lincoln, Nebraska. I would like to invite you to be a part of this outstanding event.

The contest will begin about 11:30 a.m. and will run to approximately 6:00 p.m. Each band will be allowed twelve (12) minutes for its presentation. The time includes getting on and off the field. A warm-up time and warm-up field will also be provided for each band.

We will use the new NSBA six judge format for adjudication. Superior or Participant trophies will be awarded to all bands. We offer the option for auxiliary units or drum majors to be adjudicated by a seventh judge and a trophy or plaque presented in this area.

The entry fee for the contest is $100.00 per band or $115.00 if auxiliary units are to be adjudicated. I sincerely hope you will enter your band in what has become an outstanding yearly competition for marching bands.

In addition to the four Lincoln Public Schools bands, we can accept only thirteen bands. When we have received thirteen entry forms, we will halt the entries. Please indicate on the enclosed form your desire to participate in the contest on October 13, 2001, and return it along with your entry fee by September 7, 2001.

Sincerely yours,

Richard O. Scott
Supervisor of Music

ENTRY FORM
FOR THE LINCOLN PUBLIC SCHOOLS
INVITATIONAL MARCHING BAND CONTEST
OCTOBER 13, 2001

Name of School: _____

Phone Numbers: (School) _____ (Home) _____

E-Mail_____

Band Director's Name: _____

Band Classification (i.e.: AA-A): _____ Number in Marching Band: _____

Type of Auxiliary Unit to be adjudicated: _____

_____ Yes, I would like to participate.

      _____ Band entry fee enclosed ($100.00)

      _____ Band, plus auxiliary unit entry fee enclosed ($115.00)

_____ Sorry, I am unable to participate. Please contact me again next year.

* Make your check payable to: Lincoln Public Schools.
* Return this form and entry fee check to: Richard O. Scott; Supervisor of Music
  Lincoln Public Schools; PO Box 82889; Lincoln, NE 68501.
* You will be notified by September 28, 2001 of times and other information.

2001 LPS INVITATIONAL MARCHING BAND CONTEST
PROGRAM INFORMATION SHEET
(Please type.)

SCHOOL _____

CITY_____School Enrollment_____

PRINCIPAL _____

BAND DIRECTOR_____

AUXILIARY UNIT NAME_____

AUXILIARY UNIT ADVISOR_____

DRUM MAJORS   _____

                   _____

                   _____

                   _____

PROGRAM SELECTIONS   **COMPOSER/ARRANGER**

_____

_____

_____

_____

Past Awards and Travel

_____

_____

_____

_____

Please return this form no later than October 1, 2001 to: **Richard Scott**
Supervisor of Music
Lincoln Public Schools
P.O. Box 82889
Lincoln, NE 68501

INSTRUCTIONS AND INFORMATION FOR THE
LINCOLN PUBLIC SCHOOLS INVITATIONAL MARCHING BAND CONTEST

1. The contest will begin at 11:30 a.m. at Seacrest Field, 75th and "A" Street on October 13, 2001. Upon your arrival, please check in with Mr. Richard Scott, Music Supervisor.

2. A student host will meet you 5 minutes before your rehearsal time to take you to the rehearsal area.

3. Each band will be allowed 15 minutes for final warm-up and 15 minutes for performance.

4. Each band will assemble in the South end-zone of Seacrest Field.

5. A warm-up area will be provided directly South of Lincoln East High School and each band may use the area for 15 minutes – 45 minutes before scheduled contest time. A runner will lead you to the south side of the Stadium and into the south end zone.

6. Seven judges will adjudicate; 6 for the bands and 1 for auxiliary units.

7. An award will be presented to each Division I (Superior) winner regardless of class, but no overall class winner will be chosen. Awards will be presented at the end of class A & AA classifications. All bands will receive an award.

8. An award will be presented to the auxiliary units participating, if the director opted to have the unit adjudicated.

9. Please plan to stay until after the awards presentation for your class.

10. Judges will use the Nebraska State Bandmasters Association official marching band ballots to adjudicate the contest (see enclosures).

11. Photographs and videotapes will be available for purchase.

12. All bands are asked to go to the photography stage for a group photo following your performance. Photographs may be ordered at that time.

13. The contest will be held regardless of the weather conditions.

14. The stadium concession stand will be open starting at 11:00 a.m.

15. Buses, vans and cars should park in the West Parking Lot next to the stadium.

16. There will be a $4.00 admission fee for spectators. ($1.00 for children 12 and under and $1.00 for Golden Card holders.)

PERFORMANCE
and
WARM-UP SCHEDULE
LPS Marching Band Contest
October 13, 2001

SCHOOL	CLASS	WARM-UP	PERFORMANCE
East Butler	C	10:45	11:30
Palmyra	C	11:00	11:45
Nemaha Valley	C	11:15	12:00
Pawnee City	C	11:30	12:15
Fillmore Central	B	11:45	12:30
Wahoo Neumann	B	12:00	12:45
Platteview	B	12:15	1:00
Norris	A	12:30	1:15
Waverly	A	12:45	1:30
Beatrice	A	1:00	1:45
		AWARDS PRESENTATION	2:25
Grand Island	AA	2:00	2:45
Pius X	AA	2:15	3:00
East	AA	2:30	3:15
Papillion-LaVista	AA	2:45	3:30
Lincoln High	AA	3:00	3:45
Kearney	AA	3:15	4:00
Southeast	AA	3:30	4:15
Hastings	AA	3:45	4:30
Northeast	AA	4:00	4:45
		AWARDS PRESENTATION	5:25

Appendix C: District Surveys and Strategic Plan Examples

High School Teacher Questionnaire

(May 1994)

Please check to indicate whether you teach vocal or instrumental music:

___ Vocal   ___ Instrumental

This questionnaire provides opportunity for you to help in the Music SIM study by giving information and opinions about elements of the LPS music program. The information will be used to help establish direction for the music program over the next several years. Your name is <u>not</u> required on this form and your participation, while encouraged, is voluntary. Please return your completed questionnaire to LPSDO, Box 52 by May 20th. If you have questions please feel free to call Richard Scott (1631) or Bob Reineke (1792).

SECTION I

For each question on this and succeeding pages provide information as requested.

1. Are there special needs students in your classes? ___ Yes ___ No
   If yes, are there additional support? Describe (briefly)
   _____
   _____

2. What kind of support do you need to teach special needs students? Describe (briefly):
   _____
   _____

3. Do you feel prepared to teach special needs student? ___ Yes ___ No
   [If no, skip to the next question 5]

4. With what needs?(Check all that apply)

_____ Visually Handicapped
_____ Hearing impaired
_____ Speech Language Impaired
_____ Mentally Handicapped
_____ Behaviorally Disordered
_____ Specific Learning Disabled
_____ Orthopedically Impaired

5. Do you need additional training for teaching special needs students? ___ Yes ___ No

6. How much time do you spend giving instruction to students? (Minutes per week per grade)

Grade PreK _____   3 _____   7 _____   10 _____
Grade K _____   4 _____   8 _____   11 _____
Grade 1 _____   5 _____   9 _____   12 _____
Grade 2 _____   6 _____

7. How much time before or after school do students spend with you receiving instruction? (Minutes per week per grade)

Grade PreK _____   3 _____   7 _____   10 _____
Grade K _____   4 _____   8 _____   11 _____
Grade 1 _____   5 _____   9 _____   12 _____
Grade 2 _____   6 _____

8. When you document behaviors of students, do you do so during (Check all that apply):
___ instruction time   ___ plan time   ___ personal time

9. How many students do you formally evaluate? (i.e., report cards) _____

SECTION II

Yes	No	N/A		
—	—	—	1.	Does the amount of reimbursement you receive from the district influence your decision to attend professional conventions?
—	—	—	2.	Do you have a paid accompanist for practices?
—	—	—	3.	Do you have a paid accompanist for programs?
—	—	—	4.	Should more district administrators be provided for music?
—	—	—	5.	Should more use be made of team teaching among music staff?
—	—	—	6.	Do you have access to "paras" for clerical support?
—	—	—	7.	Are grade levels (K to grade 5 or 6) scheduled consecutively in your building?
—	—	—	8.	Should this kind of scheduling occur?

— — —	9.	Do you have input into scheduling?
— — —	10.	Would an additional period (8 periods) allow more students to continue participation in your program?
— — —	11.	Would you be interested in exploring other scheduling options? (e.g. 4 period day)
— — —	12.	Is there scheduled time for inter-departmental planning in your building?
— — —	13.	Would you use a series book in your middle school music classes?
— — —	14.	Do you use central library materials?
— — —	15.	Would you like to see a standard set of supplemental instructional materials in each building?
— — —	16.	Should there be opportunities to augment a standard set of equipment through a district bank?
— — —	17.	Should there be a standard set of instruments placed in each building?
— — —	18.	Is there sufficient equipment to serve all students?

IF YOU HAVE COMMENTS ON ANY OF THE ABOVE, LIST THEM IN THE COMMENTS
SECTION ON THE LAST PAGE
(PLEASE INCLUDE THE SECTION AND QUESTION NUMBER)

SECTION III
LPS MUSIC GOALS RATING

Please rate the 15 LPS Music Goals in terms of the <u>importance</u> that you attach to each (at your level), and to what <u>degree you currently</u> address these goals in your curriculum.

Your response options are:

IMPORTANCE:		DEGREE ADDRESSED:
<u>V</u>ery <u>I</u>mportant - 1 <u>I</u>mportant - 2		<u>F</u>requently - 1
<u>S</u>omewhat <u>I</u>mportant - 3 <u>N</u>ot <u>I</u>mportant - 4		<u>O</u>ccasionally - 2 <u>S</u>eldom - 3

LPS Music Goals

Importance				Goals	Degree Addressed in Curriculum		
<u>VI</u>	<u>I</u>	<u>SI</u>	<u>NI</u>		<u>F</u>	<u>O</u>	<u>S</u>
1	2	3	4	1. Perform music alone and with others;	1	2	3
1	2	3	4	2. Improvise and compose music;	1	2	3
1	2	3	4	3. Use the vocabulary and notation of music	1	2	3
1	2	3	4	4. Respond to music aesthetically, intellectually, and emotionally;	1	2	3
1	2	3	4	5. Think critically and creatively;	1	2	3

1 2 3 4		6.	Become acquainted with a wide variety of music, including diverse musical styles representing cultures from throughout the world;	1	2	3
1 2 3 4		7.	Understand the uses and influences of music in the lives of human beings;	1	2	3
1 2 3 4		8.	Understand the uses and influences of technology in music;	1	2	3
1 2 3 4		9.	Make aesthetic judgments based on critical listening and analysis;	1	2	3
1 2 3 4		10.	Apply leadership and self-discipline skills to solve problems;	1	2	3
1 2 3 4		11.	Develop and integrate a multi-sensory approach (aural, visual, kinesthetic, and tactile skills) to enhance learning;	1	2	3
1 2 3 4		12.	Develop a commitment to music;	1	2	3
1 2 3 4		13.	Develop a positive self-image;	1	2	3
1 2 3 4		14.	Support the musical life of the community community and encourage others to do so;	1	2	3
1 2 3 4		15.	Continue their musical learning and enjoyment independently.	1	2	3

SECTION IV

Table (Equipment)

1. The table below contains a list of supplemental equipment that might be used as part of the music program. For each piece, please indicate by placing an "x" in the appropriate space if the equipment is desired, <u>check</u> if it is adequate, and <u>check</u> if you believe it should be provided by central office or the building.

	Desired	Adequate	Building	Provided by Central Office	Teacher	PTO
Electronic Keyboards	____	____	____	____	____	____
Stereo System	____	____	____	____	____	____
Tapes/Cassettes	____	____	____	____	____	____
C/D Player	____	____	____	____	____	____
CDs	____	____	____	____	____	____
Sound System	____	____	____	____	____	____
VCR	____	____	____	____	____	____
Video Tapes	____	____	____	____	____	____
Computer	____	____	____	____	____	____
Software	____	____	____	____	____	____
Instructional Materials	____	____	____	____	____	____
Equipment (chairs, etc.)	____	____	____	____	____	____
Pitched Instruments	____	____	____	____	____	____
Non-pitched Instruments	____	____	____	____	____	____
Other _____	____	____	____	____	____	____

2. What resources do you use from LPSDO?

_____

_____

3. What resources should be added to LPSDO?

_____

_____

4.   What resources should be added to your building?

_____

_____

SECTION V

Please evaluate your students on the following MENC subject matter achievements:

(Response Options)

1-Few Students	4-Most Students
2-Less than 1/2	3-More than 1/2
5-N/A	

By the end of **_GRADE 12_**, the student can (circle appropriate response for each):

Achievement	Students Achieving				
Demonstrate good posture and breath control............................	1	2	3	4	5
Sing/play with a free tone and accurate pitch throughout their ranges..	1	2	3	4	5
Interpret correctly pitches, rhythms, and other notational symbols through singing/playing	1	2	3	4	5
Sing/play accurately an appropriate part in an ensemble, with or without accompaniment..	1	2	3	4	5
Demonstrate improved skill at reading music and growth in musicianship	1	2	3	4	5
Sing/play a repertoire of choral literature of a varied nature	1	2	3	4	5
Sing/play from memory some of the music performed publicly by the ensemble	1	2	3	4	5
Demonstrate a knowledge of music notation and symbols...........	1	2	3	4	5
Discuss the historical and cultural background of the works being rehearsed	1	2	3	4	5
Evaluate the quality of performances by choral/instrumental ensembles	1	2	3	4	5

High School students who participate in choral/instrumental ensembles demonstrate:

An enjoyment in singing/playing..	1	2	3	4	5
A respect for quality music...	1	2	3	4	5
A respect for the skilled performance of music...........................	1	2	3	4	5
A commitment to singing/playing well	1	2	3	4	5
A commitment to their ensemble...	1	2	3	4	5
A personal aesthetic response to the music performed and heard	1	2	3	4	5

Please indicate comments on back page.

120 • Handbook for Music Supervision

Los Angeles Unified School District
ARTS EDUCATION OPERATIONAL PLAN

Goal I	Provide a substantive program of curriculum, instruction, and assessment in dance, music, theatre, and visual arts in grades K–12.

OBJECTIVE A   Develop and obtain curriculum and instructional resources for teaching and learning in the arts that are cohesive and aligned to one another.

STRATEGIES	IMPLEMENTATION TASKS	IMPLEMENTATION YEAR	1999-2000 BUDGET
1. Create District Learning Standards in the Arts describing what students should know and be able to do in dance, music, theatre and visual arts.	• Convene task force to write District Arts Standards based on state and national standards documents. • Adopt District Arts Standards as part of core curriculum. • Disseminate Standards to schools. • Provide orientation meetings for all teachers.	1997-1998 March 1998 May 1998 On-going	On-going
2. Align the District Elementary Course of Study and Secondary Guidelines for Instruction in the Arts to the arts standards.	• District arts staff align Elementary Course of Study and Secondary Guidelines for Instruction to Arts Standards. • Circulate draft versions of Course of Study and Guidelines for Instruction for comment and revision. • Approve revised Elementary Course of Study and Secondary Guidelines for Instruction. • Disseminate final versions of curriculum to schools.	1998-1999 Spring 1999 Fall 1999 Fall 1999	In-kind
3. Develop instructional strategies for all grade levels based on the Arts Standards for dance, music, theatre and visual arts that integrate the arts with District literacy goals.	• Create Standards-Based Instructional Models that provide teacher-created examples for each Arts Standard • District arts staff develop and identify dance, music, theatre and visual arts lessons that integrate with other curricular areas. • Develop, circulate, revise and adopt grade-level activities and assessments for elementary and secondary classes. • Work with other District unit personnel to develop and communicate strategies for integration of the arts into other content areas.	1998-1999 1999-2000 1999-2000 On-going	In-kind In-kind In-kind In-kind

Appendix C: District Surveys and Strategic Plan Examples • 121

Los Angeles Unified School District
ARTS EDUCATION OPERATIONAL PLAN

Goal I   Provide a substantive program of curriculum, instruction, and assessment in dance, music, theatre, and visual arts in grades K–12.

Objective D   Institute a one year of performing and visual arts requirement for middle school students and an arts graduation requirement for senior high school students.

Strategies	Implementation Tasks	Implementation Year	1999-2000 Budget
1. Develop requirements and seek approval from the Board of Education.	• Develop a senior high school graduation requirement and submit to Board of Education for approval.	1998-1999	In-kind
	• Meet with District administration to develop an arts requirement for middle school students.	1999-2000	In-kind
	• Submit a middle school arts requirement for Board of Education approval.	Spring 2000	In-kind
	• Meet with District administration to define arts for elementary schools.	2001-2002	
2. Develop sequential arts courses to fulfill graduation requirements.	• Meet with a committee of secondary arts teachers to develop strategies for planning instructional matrixes across the four arts disciplines that fulfill specific arts graduation requirements.	1999-2000	In-kind
	• Provide secondary schools with descriptions of sequential arts courses that fulfill graduation requirements in the arts.	1999-2000	In-kind
3. Expand offerings for advanced placement and arts honors courses in senior high schools.	• Meet with arts teachers to provide orientation for the need to expand advanced placement and arts honors courses in senior high schools.	1998-2000	In-kind

Los Angeles Unified School District
ARTS EDUCATION OPERATIONAL PLAN

Goal I   Provide a substantive program of curriculum, instruction, and assessment in dance, music, theatre, and visual arts in grades K–12.

OBJECTIVE F   Provide sufficient staff, office space and equipment to support the District arts education program.

STRATEGIES	IMPLEMENTATION TASKS	IMPLEMENTATION YEAR	1999–2000 BUDGET
2. Assess annually staff and budget needs for the District Performing and Visual Arts Unit.	• Provide 3,750 more instruments for elementary music program including new VH-1 programs (150 programs x 25 instruments x $311)	July 1999 (one-time)	$1,166,250
	• Provide one music adviser to coordinate District-wide festivals including mariachi and jazz, special programs and provide assistance to middle school music programs.	1999–2000 On-going	$66,386
	• Provide 1 elementary music specialist position to evaluate elementary traveling music teachers, oversee program, and assist with assessment development. (MST 37G)	1999–2000 On-going	$88,776
	• Provide one visual arts adviser to coordinate visual arts special programs and provide assistance to senior high school visual arts programs.	1999–2000 On-going	$66,386
	• Provide 2 clerical positions for payroll reporting and secretarial duties for Performing and Visual Arts Unit.	1999–2000 On-going	$81,390
	• Provide a stock clerk for the music office to oversee resource library and assist with assignment of music instruments to schools.	1999–2000 On-going	$21,873
	• Provide supplies and phone service for Performing and Visual Arts Unit.	1999–2000 On-going	$78,500
	• Provide computer hardware and software for Performing and Visual Arts Unit.	1999–2000 (one-time)	$22,000 (one time)
	• Provide conference and meeting attendance for performing and visual arts unit staff. (21 x $600)	(1999–2000) On-going	$12,600
	• Provide matching funds for grants from California Arts Council and California Department of Education.	1999–2002 (3 year grants)	$60,000

Appendix D: District Curricula

5th Grade General Music

Program Goal 5.1: Singing, alone and with others, a varied repertoire of music.

Outcomes The learner will:	Indicators/Objectives The learner will:	Key Content/Key Ideas	Instructional Strategies	Assessment
5.1.1 Sing with a supported tone.	A. Discriminate between supported and non-supported tones.	• Recognize appropriately supported singing	• Listening examples • T Chart • Teacher modeling • Student modeling • Music literature – Expository • Reading • Video	• Performance assessment • Listening assessment • Video tape • Rubric • Teacher observation • Journaling • Self assessment
5.1.2 Sing with accurate vowel sounds.	A. Demonstrate accurate vowel shapes/sounds.	• Vowel purity • Placement of diphthongs		
5.1.3 Sing in harmony.	A. Sing the harmony with a provided melody in a 2-part setting.	• Harmony in 3rd's or 6th's • Counter-melody • Descant • Melody vs. harmony		

Program Goal 5.2: Performing on instruments, alone and with others, a varied repertoire of music.

Outcomes The learner will:	Indicators/Objectives The learner will:	Key Content/Key Ideas	Instructional Strategies	Assessment
5.2.1 Perform short songs.	A. Perform a short song alone or with others.	• Perform with accurate pitch and technique	• Barred instruments • Recorders • Small groups • Large group • Solos • Autoharp/omnichord • Piano	• Performance assessment • Video tape • Checklist • Rubric • Journaling • Self assessment • Teacher observation
5.2.2 Perform accompaniments.	A. Play a simple harmonic accompaniment. B. Play a simple melodic accompaniment.	• I, IV, V harmonization • Countermelody • Melodic ostinato		

Program Goal 5.3: Improvising melodies, variations, and accompaniments.

Outcomes The learner will:	Indicators/Objectives The learner will:	Key Content/Key Ideas	Instructional Strategies	Assessment
5.3.1 Improvise rhythms.	A. Create 2 measure rhythmic answers to given 2 measure rhythmic questions.	• Rhythmic repetition • Contrast	• Teacher question – student answer • Un-pitched instruments • Body percussion • Pitched instruments • Singing • Guided practice • Listening examples	• Performance assessment • Checklist • Rubric • Journaling • Self assessment • Teacher observation
5.3.2 Improvise melodies.	A. Create 2 measure melodic answers to given 2 measure melodic questions.	• Melodic repetition • Contrast		

Program Goal 5.4: Composing and arranging music within specified guidelines.

Outcomes The learner will:	Indicators/Objectives The learner will:	Key Content/Key Ideas	Instructional Strategies	Assessment
5.4.1 Compose melodies within specified guidelines.	A. Compose melodies demonstrating stepwise and skipping movement. B. Compose melodies with contrasting sections.	• Diatonic intervals • Step/skip • Compose a "B" section to a given "A" section	• Elevated tone bells • Recorders • Barred instruments • Staff notation • Guided practice • Cooperative learning • Teacher modeling • Direct instruction • Composition criteria	• Performance assessment • Written product • Rubric • Checklist • Self assessment

Program Goal 5.5: Reading and notating music.

Outcomes The learner will:	Indicators/Objectives The learner will:	Key Content/Key Ideas	Instructional Strategies	Assessment
5.5.1 Demonstrate rhythm reading skills.	A. Read, notate and perform rhythms.	• Quarter note, quarter rest, eighth note pairs, half note, half rest, dotted half note, whole note and whole rest, sixteenth notes in 2/4, 3/4 and 4/4 meters	• Sight-reading examples (expository text) • Echo clapping • Games • Flashcards • Cooperative learning: inside/outside circle	• Listening assessment • Written assessment • Teacher observation • EPR • Games • Performance assessment
5.5.2 Demonstrate note reading skills on the staff.	A. Identify and sing or play a major scale. B. Identify and sing or play intervals on the treble staff.	• Whole and half steps • Intervals of a major scale	• Bar instruments • Dry erase boards • Floor staff • Music literature • Warm-up exercises • Group work	
5.5.3 Identify symbols and traditional musical terms.	A. Identify music symbols and terms.	• Staff, treble clef, *f, p,* <, >, measure, bar line, double bar line, repeat sign, fermata, slur, staccato, tie, D.S., D.C., legato, allegro and largo, *pp, ff, mp, mf,* flat, sharp, natural, ritardando, accelerando.	• Teacher modeling • Student modeling • Daily practice	

Program Goal 5.6: Listening to, analyzing and describing music.

Outcomes The learner will:	Indicators/Objectives The learner will:	Key Content/Key Ideas	Instructional Strategies	Assessment
5.6.1 Identify musical forms.	A. Identify the form of Theme and Variation.	• Similar/contrast • Song structure	• Listening examples • Word wall • Concept mapping • KWL • Venn diagram • Music literature • Manipulating shapes • Movement	• EPR • Journaling • Written assessment • Listening assessment • Teacher observation
5.6.2 Use appropriate terms when describing music.	A. Use musical terminology discriminately.	• Piano, forte, melody, tempo, unison, ostinato, harmony, chords, crescendo, decrescendo, pianissimo, fortissimo, mezzo piano, mezzo forte, staccato, legato, ritardando, accelerando		
5.6.3 Identify traditional choral terms.	A. Identify the terms: soprano, alto, tenor, bass, choir, solo and ensemble.	• Differences in adult voices		

Program Goal 5.7: Evaluating music and music performed.

Outcomes The learner will:	Indicators/Objectives The learner will:	Key Content/Key Ideas	Instructional Strategies	Assessment
5.7.1 Evaluate musical performances and products.	A. Develop and apply criteria for evaluating the quality of his/her own and others' performances and compositions.	■ Define quality performance ■ Evaluation of performance or product ■ Student-generated criteria	■ T-chart ■ Listening selection ■ Videos ■ Venn diagram ■ Concept web ■ Create a rubric ■ Problem solving	■ Journal ■ Rubric ■ Teacher observation of discussion ■ Written assessment ■ Self assessment

Program Goal 5.8: Understanding relationships between music, the other arts, and disciplines outside the arts.

Outcomes The learner will:	Indicators/Objectives The learner will:	Key Content/Key Ideas	Instructional Strategies	Assessment
5.8.1 Compare and contrast music and other disciplines.	A. Identify similarities and differences between music and other disciplines regarding common terminology and concepts.	■ Integrated Units ■ Texture – Social Studies ■ Tone color/Acoustics - Science ■ Form – Language Arts ■ Perspective - Art ■ Finding common terminology and defining differences/similarities	■ Word wall ■ Integrated units ■ Expository reading ■ Venn diagram ■ Story map ■ Cooperative groups	■ Teacher observation ■ Self assessment ■ Journaling

Program Goal 5.9: Understanding music in relation to history and culture.

Outcomes The learner will:	Indicators/Objectives The learner will:	Key Content/Key Ideas	Instructional Strategies	Assessment
5.9.1 Identify common musical careers.	A. Identify various musical careers.	■ Careers related to music	■ Guest speakers ■ Taped interviews ■ Expository reading ■ Listening examples ■ Venn diagram ■ T-chart ■ KWL ■ Artwork ■ Concept map	■ Teacher observation of discussion ■ Journaling ■ Student writing ■ Written assessment ■ Listening assessment
5.9.2 Identify music from various genres and historical periods.	A. Listen to and identify examples of music, instruments and composers of the Romantic era.	■ Beethoven ■ Brahms		

Appendix E: Evaluation Forms

TEXTBOOK EVALUATION

SERIES NAME

_____GRADE_____

	LOW	HIGH

1. How well do you feel that this book meets our LPS music goals? ... 1 2 3   4 5
   (I) Introduce,   (M) Maintain   (R) Reinforce

2. Rate the Song Literature....(Range, Piano Accompaniments, Age
   appropriateness, Level of difficulty, Texts, Number of songs.......) 1   2 3 4 5
   Give specific examples:

3. Rate the piano accompaniments.   1 2 3 4 5
   Give specific examples:

4. Rate the choral ensemble experiences.   1 2 3 4 5
   Give specific examples:

5. Rate the Listening Lessons.   1 2 3 4 5
   (Accuracy and presentation of materials, variety of styles and
   periods, Interactive or Passive experiences, Entire selections vs.
   excerpts, transparencies/call charts..............)
   Give specific examples:

6. Rate the Movement activities.   1 2 3 4 5

7. Rate the Creative musical experiences.   1 2 3 4 5
   (Age appropriate, concrete/abstract........)
   Give specific examples:

8. Rate the Notation experiences.   1 2 3 4 5
   Give specific examples:

9. Rate the Orff lessons.   1   2 3 4   5
    (Age appropriate, too hard/too easy,
    musical/nonmusical, ostinati.....)
    Give specific examples:

10. Rate the Kodaly lessons.   1   2 3 4   5
    (Age appropriate, text, concept development............)
    Give specific examples:

11. Rate the multicultural music experiences.   1   2 3 4   5
    (Authentic instruments, text and pronunciation, variety
    of cultures, ease of use.......)
    Give specific examples:

12. Rate the formal evaluation tools provided by the series.   1   2 3 4 5
    (On grade level, clear, easy to use............)
    Give specific examples:

13. Rate the student books/big book.   1   2 3 4   5
    (Page clarity/cluttered, appeal, student reaction.....)
    Give specific examples:

14. Rate the Teacher's manuals.   1   2 3 4   5
    (Easy to use, scripted, open ended............)
    Give specific examples:

15. Rate the compact disc recordings.   1   2 3 4   5
    (Clarity, good vocal models, orchestrations, Acoustic vs.
    electronic instruments..............)
    Give specific examples:

16. Rate the supplemental materials.   1   2 3 4 5
    (Recorder, guitar, sign, keyboard, song resource book.........)
    Give specific examples:

17. Rate how this series addresses careers.   1 2 3 4 5
     (Composing, performing, teaching, conducting.......)
     Give specific examples:

18. Rate how the series addresses the issues of technology.   1 2 3 4 5
     Give specific examples:

19. Rate how this series addresses inclusion.   1 2 3 4 5
     Give specific examples:

20. Rate how the series addresses curriculum integration.   1 2 3 4 5
     Give specific examples:

21. Rate how the series addresses equity.   1 2 3 4 5
     (Gender, age, disabilities, race...............)
     Give specific examples:

22. Rate the series.   1 2 3 4 5

Additional comments:

NAME_____

INSTRUMENTAL METHOD BOOK EVALUATION

Method Book Name_____

		LOW				HIGH

1.   Rate how and when the book introduces the "clarinet break".   1 2 3 4 5

2.   Rate the reinforcement of concepts.   1 2 3 4 5

3.   Rate the counting system. (1&2&,etc.)   1 2 3 4 5

4.   Rate the fingering charts.   1 2 3 4 5

5.   Rate the piano accompaniments.   1 2 3 4 5

6.   Rate the scale and arpeggio exercises.   1 2 3 4 5

7.   Rate the quality of the band arrangements.   1 2 3 4 5

8.   Rate when the band arrangements are introduced.   1 2 3 4 5

9.   Rate the ear training and theory exercises.   1 2 3 4 5

10.   Rate the pacing of concepts per page.   1 2 3 4 5

11.   Rate the number of recognizable melodies.   1 2 3 4 5

12.   Rate the appropriateness of keys in Book II.   1 2 3 4 5

13.   Rate the appropriateness of the first notes.   1 2 3 4 5

14.   Rate the appropriateness of the first rhythms.   1 2 3 4 5

15.   Rate the overall layout.   1 2 3 4 5

16.   Rate the teaching of articulations.   1 2 3 4 5

17.   Rate the approach to teaching percussion.   1 2 3 4 5

18.   Rate the approach to trombone slurring.   1 2 3 4 5

PLEASE PUT ADDITIONAL COMMENTS ON A SEPARATE SHEET.

NAME_____

Appendix F: Instrument Forms

ELEMENTARY INSTRUMENT LOAN AGREEMENT
Instrumental Music Department
Lincoln Public Schools
Lincoln, Nebraska

Date _____

Length of Agreement: School Year _____ ☐ Fall   ☐ Spring   ☐ Summer

Borrower's Name _____ Grade _____

Address_____ Zip _____

Phone _____

School _____ Instrumental Teacher _____

Instrument use fee is $40.00 for one (1) school year or $20.00 for half year of summer. This fee is nonrefundable.

Instrument Information

Type _____Date Borrowed_____ Date Returned_____

LPS No. _____ Make _____ Serial No. _____

Accessories _____ Mouthpiece _____

Condition of Instrument _____

_____

Replacement Value _____

I assume responsibility for the above named instrument while in the possession of my son/daughter. I also agree to pay for damages to or loss of the instrument which is the result of negligence or vandalism on the part of my child. My son/daughter and I understand that it is his/her responsibility to maintain the instrument in neat, clean and proper playing condition.

Instruments must be returned to the school before the end of the school year or upon the request of this instrumental music teacher.

Signed _____   Signed _____
Instrumental Teacher   Parent or Guardian

Date _____

Receipt No. _____

Amount _____

132

WOODWIND
REPAIR REQUEST FORM
(Lincoln Public Schools)

School_____Instructor_____

Date:_____/_____/_____

Instrument_____Serial/LPS#_____

Circle items to be repaired.

1. **SOLDER: Braces. Key guard.**

2. **PADS: Complete repad.**   Register, <u>High</u> F#, F, E, Eb, D, <u>Mid</u> C#,C, B, alt. B,
                                    Bb, A, G#, G, F#, alt. F#, F, E,
                                    <u>Low</u> D#/Eb, D, C#, C, B, Bb, A

3. **PIN CRACKS**

4. **KEYS: Bent. Loose. Braze.**

5. **POST: Loose. Solder.**

6. **JOINTS: Recork. Repair.**

7. **SPRINGS: Adjust tension. Replace/ Remove**

8. **ACTION: Adjust. Regulate.**

9. **OVERHAUL (Requires Music Supervisor's Approval)**

10. **CASE REPAIR: New handle. Hinge. Latch. Corner brackets.**

ADDITIONAL REPAIRS or COMMENTS:

_____

_____

_____

Please complete, put white copy in case with instrument, keep yellow and pink copies, and send goldenrod copy to music office (Box #29).

When repair is completed and instrument returned to your school, please complete this portion and send pink copy and the vendor's invoice to the music office.

This instrument was returned on ____/____/____. _____
                                                        Teacher's Signature

Amount of Repair $_____

STRING
REPAIR REQUEST FORM
(Lincoln Public Schools)

School: _____ Instructor: _____

Date:____/____/____

Instrument: _____Scratch/LPS #: _____

Instructions: Circle items(s) to be repaired

1. **Pegs:** Replace – Fit and Adjust – Repair Gears

2. **Fingerboard:** Reglue – Replace Nut

3. **Neck:** Reset

4. **Scroll:** Glue and Reinforce

5. **Tailpiece:** Replace

6. **Bridge:** Replace – Refit

7. **Sound Post:** Reset – Replace

8. **End Pin:** Replace – Straighten – Rethread Screw

9. **Saddle:** Replace – Repair

10. **Repair Cracks in** _____

11. **Repair Open Seams**

12. **Repair/Replace Neck Block/Tail Block**

ADDITIONAL REPAIRS OR COMMENTS:

_____

_____

_____

Please complete, put white copy in case with instrument, keep yellow and pink copies, and send goldenrod copy to music office (Box #29).

When repair is completed and instrument returned to your school, please complete this portion and send pink copy and the vendor's invoice to the music office.

This instrument was returned on ____/____/____. _____

Teacher's Signature

Amount of Repair $_____

BRASS
REPAIR REQUEST FORM
(Lincoln Public Schools)

School: _____   Instructor: _____

Date:___/___/___

Instrument: _____   Serial/LPS #: _____

Instructions: Circle item(s) to be repaired:

1.	Valves:	Repair	Clean	Restring	Align
		Replace corks and felts			
2.	Slides:	Draw	Remove Dent	Clean	Tighten
		Solder	Straighten		
3.	Water Key:	Replace spring		Recork	Repair/Replace
4.	*Dents:	Remove dents			
5.	Solder:	All leaks	Slides	Braces	Patch cracks
6.	Mouthpiece:	Pull	Straighten		
7.	Mouthpipe:	Solder	Patch	Replace	Straighten
8.	Chemical Bath				
9.	Case - Repair:	Handle	Hinges	Clasps	Corners

*Requires Music Supervisor's Approval

ADDITIONAL REPAIRS or COMMENTS:

_____

_____

_____

_____

Please complete, put white copy in case with instrument, keep yellow and pink copies, and send goldenrod copy to music office (Box #29).

When repair is completed and instrument returned to your school, please complete this portion and send pink copy and the vendor's invoice to the music office.

This instrument was returned on ___/___/___. _____
                                                Teacher's Signature

Amount of Repair $_____

PERCUSSION
REPAIR REQUEST FORM
(Lincoln Public Schools)

School_____Instructor_____

Date:_____/_____/_____

Instrument_____Serial/LPS#_____

Circle items to be repaired:

1. Snares: Repair   Replace

2. Snare adjuster: Repair   Replace

3. Hoop: Repair   Replace

4. Damper   Repair   Replace

5. Vibraphone   Repair/Replace motor

ADDITIONAL REPAIRS or COMMENTS:

_____

_____

_____

_____

Please complete, attach white copy to instrument, keep yellow and pink copies, and send goldenrod copy to music office (Box#29).

When repair is completed and instrument returned to your school, please complete this portion and send pink copy and the vendor's invoice to the music office.

This instrument was returned on _____/_____/_____.   _____
                                                              Teacher's Signature

Amount of Repair $_____